From Wall Street to Main Street

From Wall Street to Main Street

Why America Is Being Destroyed from Within

REGINALD F. DAVIS

RESOURCE *Publications* • Eugene, Oregon

FROM WALL STREET TO MAIN STREET
Why America Is Being Destroyed from Within

Copyright © 2013 Reginald F. Davis. All rights reserved. Except for brief quotations in critical publications or reviews, no part of this book may be reproduced in any manner without prior written permission from the publisher. Write: Permissions, Wipf and Stock Publishers, 199 W. 8th Ave., Suite 3, Eugene, OR 97401.

Resource Publications
An Imprint of Wipf and Stock Publishers
199 W. 8th Ave., Suite 3
Eugene, OR 97401

www.wipfandstock.com

ISBN 13: 978-1-62564-244-8

Manufactured in the U.S.A.

Contents

Preface *vii*

Acknowledgments *xxi*

ONE   Created for a Great Purpose   1

TWO   Freedom without Responsibility   18

THREE   The Enemy Who Deceives Us   37

FOUR   Blind and Don't Know It   53

FIVE   The Toll of Gun Violence   72

SIX   When a Nation Forgets God   84

SEVEN   Lost Values   101

Conclusion:
There Is Hope for America   113

Bibliography   123

Preface

Apart from God the whole thing is meaningless and might
as well not have been. Apart from God and his forgiveness
nationality and even Christianity particularized in a nation
become destructive rather than creative.

—H. RICHARD NIEBUHR

There is an alarming trend in America that parallels the destruction of other nations. America is being destroyed from within. Unless America comes back to God and reorders its priorities, future generations will ask, "Why has the mighty fallen?" The greed of the plutocrats and the oligarchs on Wall Street, the immorality on Main Street, massive national debt, partisan bickering among politicians, the dysfunction of our schools, the silence of many churches, and the culture that feels no shame all point to the downward spiral and decay of America. When we read Gibbon's *The History of the Decline and Fall of the Roman Empire* (originally published in 6 volumes beginning in 1776 and now available as an abridged Penguin Classic), and look at America today, the parallels are frightening. For example, a primary reason for Rome's fall was widespread corruption; the leaders of Rome lined their own pockets until they bankrupted the

Preface

empire. They looked out for themselves and not the interest of the empire. Immorality, promiscuity, sexual perversion, high divorce rates, disrespect and rebellion against parents, criminal activity in high and low places, and an overall loss of responsibility in the culture contributed to the decline and fall of the Roman Empire. We see similar trends in America.

America's moral and spiritual deterioration springs from its moral toxicity. Americans from every class, creed, and color are living in darkness; they lack moral convictions and fail to comprehend the consequences of their actions. God will judge America's immorality just as God has judged the immorality of other powerful nations. Further, if God does not bring judgment to America, then God must apologize for bringing judgment on other nations. As William Wilberforce wrote in *Real Christianity*,

> The problems we face as a society should be viewed as spiritual problems rather than merely political and economic issues. This is a perspective that does not even appear to be considered by the media. What can we expect from the kinds of solutions they offer? Certainly they would only produce transient progress, not fundamental change. What needs to happen is that every effort must be made to raise the standards of public morality in our nation. This is a responsibility that falls especially on people who have influence and power, whether political or financial.[1]

Unless Americans repent, no political party, legislation, or economic plan can save the nation. Removing

---

1. Wilberforce, *Real Christianity*, 160.

Preface

God from public and private institutions is a serious sin because "Unless the Lord builds the house, they labor in vain who build it; unless the Lord guards the city, the watchman stays awake in vain" (Ps 127:1). We cannot spend enough money for homeland security when we have abandoned core spiritual values that promote respect, responsibility, morality and civility. When these values have dried up in a nation, the nation topples and falls.

America is in deep trouble. What is more disturbing is the staggering biblical illiteracy in a country that considers itself Christian. We seem to understand America was founded on biblical principles, but this country has moved so far away from biblical principles that we have become more accurately a pagan nation. Political correctness demands that we don't offend others. Our nation has embraced a multi-cultural, multi-religious identity. No single God will be tolerated in public places. Therefore, many Americans have elected to privatize God and allow lesser gods to exist in public places. There is nothing wrong with diversity and freedom of expression, but when the true and living God has been placed alongside lesser gods, we have sunk to idolatry. God will not share his glory and demonstrated His displeasure on Israel when the Israelites worshiped false gods.

The profound biblical illiteracy among Christians is also disturbing. Many Christians have never read and meditated on God's word; this explains in part why they are losing battles in a world that is getting more complex, cynical, and dangerous. The knowledge that would set people and communities free is given low to no priority. The pressures of home, work, and other competing interests have created functionally illiterate Christians who are out of touch with spirituality and who are not paying attention to who they are. Far too many of God's people are ill-prepared to deal with our society's issues of race, culture, religious and sexual pluralism, natural disasters, a declining democracy, and the growing threat to us all: terrorism. Too many of God's people are dealing with our cultural crises through chemical dependency, excessive consumerism, sexual liberalism, religious and ethical quietism, and other forms of escapism—all of which leaves them broken and unsatisfied. God's people—who should be the light of the world—are in bondage and cannot find a way out. Isaiah and Hosea, the prophets of old, echo a truism from antiquity: "My people have gone into captivity because they have no knowledge . . . " (Isa 5:13) and "my people are destroyed for a lack of knowledge . . . " (Hos 4:6). How can we "Be ready to give an answer to everyone that ask [us] a reason of the hope that is in [us] with meekness and fear" (1 Pet 3:15) when we don't know what this hope is? Biblical illiteracy is a primary problem among contemporary American Christians.

William Wilberforce said, "This is one reason why the diligent study of the Bible is so important. It is here that God has given us the instruction we need to be able to tell right from wrong and truth from error. Without understanding its principles and precepts, we become victims of our own subjectivity"[2] Many people come *to* church, but they are not *of* the church. Many join the church, but they never really join Jesus Christ. How can they know Christ when they never abide in his word?

2. Ibid., 24.

Preface

Going to church for many Christians is a social affair; it is a place to belong, a place to identify with others without ever really identifying with Christ. Held captive by a culture that has blinded their spiritual vision, American Christians are failing to form a saving, personal relationship with Jesus Christ.

Without biblical literacy and without a personal relationship with Christ, American Christians are incapable of striking a blow for the Kingdom of God. William Wilberforce called these people "cultural Christians." By this he means society has given these Christians a set of cultural values that are out of sync with the word of God. Society has taught them to break with the past and live in the present, but that present is rife with theories and ideas that push them further and further away from God and his kingdom. It is true we should break from traditions of sin, evil, oppression, and spiritual blindness, but we should never break from the tradition of our faith that taught us how to love and live responsibly before God and one another. The Apostle Paul reminds us, "Stand fast and hold the traditions which you were taught, whether by word or our epistle" (2 Thess 2:15). We must hold fast to the traditions of our faith that taught us about God and His righteousness and our responsibility to do the will of God on earth as it is in heaven.

Unfortunately today many Christians are more concerned about political correctness than about spiritual correctness, more concerned about being safe than about being saved, more concerned about rights than about righteousness. To do the God's will, we must look through the lenses of God's word rather than through the lenses of the culture around us. We must work to transform the

Preface

culture and not allow the culture to transform us. Too many of God's people have become spiritually lethargic and sleepy. Too many have disconnected themselves from spiritual values that brought us closer to one another and morally challenged those who ruled over us. If we forget what we have learned in the past, we will not know how to cope in the present and face challenges in the future. We must build from the past traditions of our faith and not reinvent the wheel to appease the culture around us. The collapse of spiritual values on the one hand and rapid changes on the other have caused God's people to become disoriented. Look at the vast number of young people who are not connected to the church and turn to other outlets for answers. Look at how the postmodern church has disconnected itself from the Kingdom of God and become like other social institutions. The postmodern church has almost given up its spiritual power and authority; this explains why we have not been able to transform the culture around us. Just like Adam gave up his authority in the garden of Eden and subjected himself to the authority of the enemy, the postmodern church has relinquished its power. For this reason many of God's people are unable to navigate life's difficult maze. Many people have no idea or understanding of the spiritual warfare that is taking place in our world. They have no idea how important it is for us to pay attention to who we are and the alienated knowledge we are embracing.

Alienated knowledge consists of information, theories, ideas, suggestions, and practices that cause us to abandon core spiritual values that Jesus and the prophets taught us. The truth of what Jesus and the prophets taught us can break through a world of false values to help us see the eternal light, which is often eclipsed by the culture of humanism. Humanism explains our human condition in humanistic terms and believes there is no reason to postulate any truths outside of human resources. Humanists believe the human condition of delinquency, perversity, callousness, and brutality can all be explained by scientific knowledge. Scientific knowledge is a tool in assisting to understand the human condition but it is by far too inadequate to heal the human condition. Only the Spirit of God through Christ can heal our human condition, but we must know that Spirit and accept its guidance in our lives. We are in a spiritual warfare. Unless we understand spiritual truths, the road back to the eternal light is just that more distant.

To create a hopeful future, we must live out spiritual truths. Jesus, the word of God made flesh, provides the way back to God. Therefore, we should set our minds and hearts upon what Jesus Christ taught us and develop a mind like his. Scripture says, "Let this mind be in you, which was also in Christ Jesus" (Phil 2:5). Mindlessness is not of Christ. Hopelessness is not of Christ. Meaninglessness is not of Christ. God wants us to study and apply spiritual truths found in Scripture and thus become Christ-like in mind and character. Many followers of Christ across the centuries believed that Jesus holds the words of life. Jesus said, "It is the Spirit who gives life; the flesh profits nothing. The words that I speak to you are spirit, and they are life. But there are some of you who do not believe" (John 6:63–64). Many Christians fear that what Jesus taught is not socially acceptable; since they value social acceptance more than Christ, they refuse to discuss and apply the spiritual truths Christ taught. They would rather privatize it than socialize it. What Christ taught is disturbing for some but revolutionary and liberating for others. The teaching of Jesus Christ puts a face to God and reveals his love for us. When we accept what Christ taught us, we are guided back to God and those noble values and principals that can help us establish again a nation of spirituality, civility, and morality in the midst of an eroding moral infrastructure. These truths can empower us to combat the destructive forces that often leave us at different ends of the social, political, and economic spectrum.

Then, why are our nation and many of God's people confused, misguided, and destroyed? Why are they being conquered instead of being the conquerors? Why does the culture shape the Christians, but Christians aren't shaping the culture? The answer to these questions is that we are ignorant of the word of God; we do not follow his instructions or submit ourselves to his authority. Suppose we go to the doctor to find out what is wrong with our ailing bodies. Once the doctor traces the cause, recommends a course of action, and perhaps writes a prescription, the patient must fill the prescription and follow the doctor's instructions. If the patient fails to do either of these things, the body continues to ail and may eventually die. We cannot blame the doctor; the fault lies with the patient who refused to follow the doctor's instructions.

It is tragic that the prescription written for God's people is being ignored in our nation. When American Christians ignore or reject God's word, they work against themselves. Life will not go well for them for long. To reject God's word is a death sentence. Secularized or advanced knowledge has not and cannot save us. It may increase our power and mastery over nature, but it is insufficient

Preface

to give us the power of self-mastery. As Benjamin Mays stated,

> We used to believe, like Socrates, that evil and wrongdoing were based on ignorance; that men fought was because they didn't know any better; that racial prejudice was based on a lack of knowledge; that man exploited man because he needed to be enlightened. But we know that knowledge is not enough; that man can know the truth and deliberately lie, see the good and deliberately choose evil, see the light and deliberately walk in darkness, see the high road beckoning to him and deliberately choose the low road.[3]

We need something more than scientific and secularized knowledge to guide us. Second Timothy 3:7 says that we are "always learning and never able to come to the knowledge of the truth." If we don't know the truth God's word, we may be embracing a lie. As Hitler said in *Mein Kampf*, "The greater the lie, the more readily it will be believed."[4] If we neglect to study and apply the word of God to our individual and collective lives, we run the risk of embracing a lie and being destroyed.

To avoid destruction we must go back to God and adhere to the teachings of Jesus Christ and the prophets. History has proven that when we interact with one another apart from God's divine guidance, we produce nothing but mayhem and destruction. How much more can our national consciousness stand in light of what we see going on in our nation and the world? The breakdown

3. Mays, *Quotable Quotes*, 10. Vantage Press.
4. Washington, *A Testament of Hope*, 493.

Preface

in human relations, inordinate greed, the disintegration of the nuclear family, same-sex marriage, the threat of nuclear holocaust, failing schools, poverty explosion, the ecological crisis, the national debt, and a host of other national and global issues will increase as long as we continue to operate apart from God. God does not will our destruction, but God allows it. God made us with free will and because of this free will God will not force us to live life according to His word. We must choose God's way through Christ if we want life and its blessings.

Living in this age where there is acceleration in the acquisition of human knowledge, we can easily drown in news and tips that don't solve our deep and enduring problems. Therefore, we echo T. S. Eliot's question, "Where is the knowledge that is lost in information? Where is the wisdom that is lost in knowledge?"[5] Possessing the knowledge of God's word gives us wisdom. It is possible to reverse the coming judgment of God to America through the guidance of the word of God and the aid of the Holy Spirit. When the word of God came to Nineveh for its wickedness through the prophet Jonah, the people repented and said, "Who can tell if God will turn and relent, and turn away from His fierce anger, so that we may not perish" (Jonah 3:9)? Americans must repent. We don't have to be destroyed. Americans can save their families, communities, nation, and future generations from destruction if only they "will humble themselves and pray and seek my face and turn from their wicked ways, then will I hear from heaven and will forgive their sin and will heal their land" (2 Chron 7:14). Our families,

---

5. Smith, *World's Religions*, 13.

Preface

our communities, and our nation need healing, and this healing can only come through the truths that Jesus and the prophets taught us.

This book is intended to help God's people avoid destruction; I want our nation to save itself from the damnation into which it is sinking. I want to engender hope that will win others to Jesus Christ. Now more than ever before God's people must come together across race, class, and denominational lines to create a great cloud of witnesses for Jesus Christ. In the words of J. B. Phillips,

> Our society today bears all the marks of a God-starved community. There is little real moral authority because no ultimate Authority is known or acknowledged. Since there is no accepted standard of values beyond the purely material, the false god of success, the lure of glamorized sex, the love of money and the "rat-race" of business or social competition hold almost undisputed sway in the lives of many people. When the true God is unknown, that combination of awe, love, respect, admiration and wonder, which we call worship, becomes diverted toward human beings who exhibit unusual gifts in the public eye. Without the Spirit of the living God the public conscience is capricious and ill-informed.... Where there is no belief in a Purpose extending beyond this life people are inevitably oppressed by a sense of futility. And since there is no great cause for which to suffer and labor, words like "duty" and "moral obligation" have simply lost valid currency for large numbers of people.... The whole situation cries out for the restoration of real religious faith.[6]

---

6. Phillips, *God Our Contemporary*, viii.

Preface

There is hope for our dark times. Because God loves us so much, God always sends warnings to humanity before destruction. If we heed the warnings, we can change the judgment of God to the salvation of God. If we ignore the warnings, what can save us from destruction? God spoke to Ezekiel in ancient times, but he could be saying this to us today: "Say to them: 'As I live,' says the Lord God, I have no pleasure in the death of the wicked, but that the wicked turn from his way and live. Turn, turn from your evil ways! For why should you die, O house of Israel" (Ezek 33:11)?

Why should America die? Again, there is hope, but without God, we are like a ship without a sail. Recall Shakespeare's *Macbeth*: "Life's but a walking shadow, a poor player that struts and frets his hour upon the stage and then is heard no more: it is a tale told by an idiot, full of sound and fury, signifying nothing."[7]

The chapters of this book explore the factors that are causing American spiritual death and decay. Chapter 1 deals with our created purpose. We were not arbitrarily created. There is a divine purpose for our existence. Chapter 2 investigates our freedom without responsibility and how we want rights without righteousness. Chapter 3 exposes the enemy who deceives us and influences our decisions, twists our reasoning, and darkens our path toward God. Chapter 4 points out the spiritual blindness that is so pervasive in America and its influence on our culture. Chapter 5 looks at gun violence and its toll on America. Chapter 6 explores the consequences of a nation that has forgotten God. Chapter 7 points out America's

---

7. Thurman, *Jesus and the Disinherited*, 66.

Preface

lost values and how this has accelerated the moral decline of the nation. Chapter 8 is the conclusion that lifts up the hope that is still available for a morally declining nation.

Acknowledgments

I would like to acknowledge the support and prayers of the Davis family while writing this book. My wife Myrlene Davis has always been by my side to support and encourage me along the way. I want to thank my children, Isaac, Nandi, and Joel for their consistent prayers, and all the friends who have encouraged and prayed for this book. Special thanks to Leslie Andres for her outstanding copyediting. I recommend her highly. Also, special thanks to Wipf & Stock Publishers for publishing this work.

ONE

Created for a Great Purpose

"Know that the Lord, He is God; it is He who has made us, and not we ourselves; we are his people, and the sheep of his pasture." (Ps 100:3, NKJV)

Whenever God creates something, it is created for a purpose. Everything in heaven and on earth, visible and invisible is created for a purpose. God is not a purposeless God, and therefore creation is neither meaningless nor a random act of power. In Genesis 1:31 everything God created was "very good." Therefore, goodness is at the core of all creation because God is good. Creation then in its original formulation is good. Therefore, as humans we are not a joke; we are not a mistake; we are not just numbers in the census bureau. We are not just statistics in a research study. We are God's crown creation with a divine purpose. Every detail of our being is intentional. The color of our skin, the texture of our hair, the tall and shortness of our bodies, and all the differences we find among human beings were all created by God and for God's glory. We are the created intentional will of God.

From Wall Street to Main Street

In his book *The Will of God*, Leslie Weatherhead explains three wills of God that cast light on God's will for our creation. He highlights the intentional will of God, the circumstantial will of God, and the ultimate will of God. The intentional will of God means the way in which God pours himself out in goodness, such as the true father longs to do for his son. In this matter see how confused our thinking has been made by bad hymns. Here is a verse from one of them:

> Though dark my path and sad my lot,
> Let me be still and murmur not,
> But breathe the prayer divinely taught,
> "Thy will be done."

Leslie Weatherhead cannot reconcile the goodness of God and the unfortunate occurrences of evil and injustice that may victimize us and we then believe this is God's will. He raises a searching question. "What sort of a God is this, who of his own intention, not through circumstances thrust into life by ignorance, folly, or sin, but of divine intention, pours misery underserved and unhappiness, disappointment and frustration, bereavement, calamity, and ill health on his beloved children, and then asks them to look up through their tears and say, "Thy will be done?"[1]

In other words, God poured himself in our creation; and God's intentional will for us is good, delightful, and relational. We have attributes of God to see, touch, smell, taste, and think. We are endowed with the power of reason and creativity. We have within us a spiritual component, which helps us to live in relation to God and natural

---

1. Weatherhead, *The Will of God*, 14–15.

things. Because God endowed us with memory, we can bring the past to play upon the present and make decisions for the future. We can name objects, form ideas, and recall them at will. We are a marvelous piece of handiwork. In Psalm 139:14 David said, "I will praise thee; for I am fearfully and wonderfully made." Shakespeare described us beautifully through Hamlet: "What a piece of work is man, how noble in faculty, how infinite in reason. In form and moving how express and admirable and apprehension, how like a god in action, how like an angel the beauty of the world, a paragon of animals—this is man."[2]

We cannot say this about other animals such as monkeys, horses, and bears. They live by instinct. We live by reason, and this makes us higher than animals. We are the crown of God's creation. In Psalm 8:4 reminds us that God made us "A little lower than the angels and crowned us with glory and honor." Therefore, it does not matter about our skin color, our frame, our height, the texture of our hair, and other characteristics because God made it all to God's glory. Each of us is unique because God made us this way. When we reject the way we are made, we are rejecting God's particular design, color, and characteristics of our individual selves. We must accept ourselves as God made us and stop trying to remake ourselves to fit society's images of beauty. Each of us is unique and special. God took time to form each of us for his glory. We must remember that we come from God through our parents and our arrival in this world has God's particular seal on us. We are here for a reason. As Russell Kelfer writes,

2. O'Brien, *Truths Men Live By*, 53.

> You are who you are for a reason.
> You're part of an intricate plan.
> You're a precious and perfect unique design,
> called God's special woman or man.
> You look like you look for a reason.
> Our God made no mistake.
> He knit you together within the womb,
> You're just what he wanted to make.[3]

God gave each of us our own DNA and our own fingerprint. Our response to this majestic gift is to praise and glorify God. Not only are we to praise and glorify God, but also we should, as Jesus taught in Matt 22:37–40, "Love the Lord your God with all your heart, with all your soul, and with all your mind. This is the first and great commandment. And the second is like it: You shall love your neighbor as yourself. On these two commandments hang all the Law and the Prophets."

Since God created us, our relationship with God was intended to last forever. We were not created for destruction but for life. Renowned twentieth-century theologian Dietrich Bonhoeffer wrote, "God views his work and is satisfied with it; this means that God loves his work and therefore wills to preserve it. . . . God's seeing protects the world from falling back into the void, protects it from total destruction . . . and because of the way God sees his work and embraces it and does not forsake it, we live."[4] God wills life for us, and this life is to be lived and expressed within the order of divine design. In Acts 17:28 the Apostle Paul wrote, "In him, we live and move and have our being." There is no such thing as living in-

---

3. Warren, *The Purpose Driven Life*, 25.
4. Bonhoeffer, *Creation and Fall*, 25.

dependently from God. Life flows from God to us and without this flow of life, we would not exist. We can deny our dependence on God, but our existence would not be possible without God. Our existence in God is a firm foundation; to live against the order of divine design is to do so at our own peril. That which is created cannot exist on its own. It exists by the design of its Maker.

For example, since we are made in God's image and likeness, we are also endowed with the power to create. We have created many things such as combustible engines that are fueled by gasoline. If we fuel combustible engines with something other than gasoline, they malfunction. Why? The designer created the product to operate by this fuel, and it malfunctions when we replace the designer's decision with our own. Likewise, God is our Designer and Maker. Unlike combustible engines, we are created and endowed with free will. Whether we make good choices or bad, God will not overrule those choices because of our special endowment of free will. Due to the specification of our creation, God knows what it takes for us to have life and have it more abundantly. God knows what it takes to heal us and make us whole again. But, when we make the choice to go against our Creator's instructions for life, we do so at our peril. We must understand that God made us for life and has given us the manual of life. When we decide to go against the manual of God's word by ignorance or outright disobedience, we invite death upon ourselves and our children and our children's children. The downward spiral to destruction is by choice and not by design.

Having the freedom to choose is an act of being free, but freedom must be understood within a relationship given to us by God. Outside of a relationship with God it is impossible to know what freedom is because we are not self-sufficient. We are creatures dependent on our Creator. Freedom can only be conceived through the relational recognition of our Creator upon whom we are solely dependent on for our existence. Bonhoeffer writes,

> Freedom is not a quality of man, nor is it an ability, a capacity, a kind of being that somehow flares up in him. Anyone investigating man to discover freedom finds nothing of it. Why? Because freedom is not a quality which can be revealed; it is not a possession, a presence, an object, nor is it a form for existence, but a relationship and nothing else. . . . Being free means "being free for the other," because the other has bound me to him. Only in relationship with the other am I free.[5]

Our freedom is not of ourselves but bound to God. God chooses to give us freedom in Himself. Therefore, "God does not will to be free for himself but for man. God in Christ is free for man. Because he does not retain his freedom for himself, the concept of freedom only exists for us as 'being free for.' For us who live in the middle through Christ has no meaning except that we are free for God. The freedom of the Creator is proved by the fact that he allows us to be free for him, and that means nothing except that he creates his image on earth."[6]

Within the freedom God has given us, God sets boundaries we are not to cross. Creation without limitations leads to chaos and destruction. When we transgress

---

5. Ibid., 40.
6. Ibid.

Created for a Great Purpose

the boundaries God has set for us, we enter into a deep division that destroys not only ourselves but our relationship as well. Freedom and limitations go hand and hand. Without the one, the other is thrown in jeopardy. Limitations are designed to teach us responsibility. We are to be responsible within our freedom, and freedom without responsibility turns into a culturally decadent society. For instance, because we are not self-determined but dependent upon God, we cannot determine our own limitation. If we could, we would determine not to die. Death is a form of limitation we cannot control. The limitations God sets for us help to promote our salvation. Consider what kind of world it would be if there were no natural limitations placed on tyrannical leaders who destroy others without regard for life. Think of leaders such as Hitler and Mussolini who would never die. Would there be any hope of justice for those who are victims of injustice? Would there be any end to the reign of evil? Within our freedom God sets limitations for our good. Another example of limitation is gravity. Without understanding the law of gravity we would jump from high places to our untimely death. Limitations help keep us alive, but once we revolt against the limitations set by God for our good, we are in direct revolt not only against our Creator but against our very lives as well.

This brings us to Leslie Weatherhead's explanation of the second will of God, which is God's circumstantial will. "Because man's free will creates circumstances of evil that cut across God's plans, because our oneness with the great human family means that the evil among other members of it may create circumstances which disturb God's intention for us, there is a will within the will of

God, or what I call 'the circumstantial will of God.'"[7] All the evil, tyranny, war, greed, racism, and bloodshed in the world are the direct result of man's choices and God's circumstantial will. God allows these manifestations of sin because humans made a choice to rebel against the divine will. Therefore, when we want to blame God for the crimes of human history, we must think again and put the blame not on God but on ourselves. Since human free will is within the equation of our creation, we should not blame God for the manifestation of sin in the world. When we disobey, we create circumstances that work across God's intentional will for us. We frustrate God's intentional will and it takes time to work around these circumstances created by human free will to get back to God's intentional will. To achieve God's intentional will for us, God needs the human will to cooperate with the divine will. Human participation is key in achieving God's intentional will. As long as there is rebellion of the human will against the divine will, the intentional will of God for us is in a constant state of frustration. We must join God in the transformation of the world. The Jewish philosopher Martin Buber reminds us that "Man can choose God and he can reject God. . . . That man has the power to lead the world to perdition implies that he has power to lead the world to redemption . . . The fact remains that the creation of this being, man, means that God has made room for a codetermining power. . . . Has God need of man for His work? He wills to have need of man."[8]

---

7. Weatherhead, *The Will of God*, 24.
8. Buber, *Hasidism*, 108–9.

Created for a Great Purpose

For example, when God communicated the first limitation to man and woman, it was for their good. Since God views creation as "very good," it would be a fallacy to believe that God placed within us the seed of our own destruction. God created us for life and not death. What pleasure or glory can God get out of the death of his creation? Freedom is part of our creation, and with this freedom we can live in harmony with God or plant the seed of our own destruction by choosing to live out of harmony with God. According to Scripture, Adam and Eve were given a limitation, and as long as they complied with this limitation they would continue to be in harmony with God and one another. They would continue to have life. The limitation—and the consequence for disobedience—was communicated clearly to Adam. God said to Adam and Eve, "Of every tree of the garden you may freely eat; but of the tree of the knowledge of good and evil you shall not eat, for in the day that you eat of it you shall surely die" (Gen 2:16–17). Yes, this may have been a test of obedience. Within freedom there is responsibility and accountability. Bonhoeffer writes, "Certainly Adam cannot know what death, or good, or evil are, but Adam understands that in these words God confronts him and points out his limit. . . . He knows his limit because he knows God. . . . Further, he knows his life is possible only by his limit."[9] Adam is aware of his limitation. He may not know the reason for this limitation but he understands that to live is to take God at his word. But, the moment we view God's word as suspect is the moment we step into the path of destruction. We view God's word as suspect

---

9. Bonhoeffer, *Creation and Fall*, 57–58.

when we are confronted with other knowledge contrasts with the knowledge God grants us. Once this happens, we are put in a position to choose which knowledge to embrace.

Adam and Eve were enticed to reject the word of God by their own cognition. Satan, who will be discussed in another chapter, aims to divert us from the word of God and call into question its validity. Adam and Eve were presented with knowledge that contrasted with the word of God. Sadly, with this opposing knowledge they reasoned against the word of God and created alienation, evil, and destruction. Their disobedience opened their eyes to the material world of good and evil. Therefore, they hid themselves from God much as people are doing today. They now understand guilt, evil, foulness, ugliness, and death, a reality they were unaware of before. This new world is full of pain, discord, and sorrow. Because of their disobedience, God calls out to them. "Adam, where are you" (Gen 3:9)? Bonhoeffer stated, "Man is not allowed to remain in his sin alone, God speaks to him, he stops him in his flight. 'Come out of your hiding-place, from your self-reproach, your covering, your secrecy, your self-torment, from your vain remorse. . . . confess to yourself, do not lose yourself in religious despair, be yourself, Adam . . . where are you? Stand before your Creator!"[10] God wants us to be responsible, and we cannot be responsible if we are hiding from God, which is impossible to do anyway.

Like Adam and Eve, we are fleeing from God, fleeing from responsibility and accountability. We are on the

---

10. Ibid., 91.

Created for a Great Purpose

run, not realizing our running is carrying us further and further in alienation and destruction. We make excuses to avoid facing the Creator. We indulge in all kinds of self-effacing things to hide from God because we refuse to surrender to God. Like Adam, we see "This grace only as hate, as wrath, and this wrath kindles [our] own hate, [our] rebellion, and [our] will to escape from God."[11] We don't realize God is our friend, not our enemy; our heavenly Father is not our avenger. God knows our sin, and God's call to us is a call of grace. Provisions for reconciliation have already been made for us, but remaining in our sin continues to alienate us from God, who loves us and who is reaching out to us. The reaching out to fallen humanity is the reach of love. In spite of our grievous sins, Romans 5:20, teaches, "Where sin increased, grace increased all the more." We are like frightened, trapped animals that put up a ferocious struggle against rescuers. A trapped animal fears that the rescuer has come to finish him off, destroy him when the situation is just the opposite. As humans we fight against God because we fear God wants to destroy us when the situation is just the opposite. Ezekiel writes, "God has no pleasure in the death of the wicked, but that the wicked turn from his way and live" (Ezek 33:11). God is not out to destroy us. God is not a malevolent deity waiting to smoke us when we make a mistake, sin, or go astray. God is a God of love, mercy, and forgiveness.

Because Adam and Eve disobeyed, God had to allow the consequences of their action (God's circumstantial will) to manifest to teach them responsibility and obedi-

11. Ibid., 92.

ence. Leslie Weatherhead describes God's ultimate will as "The goal which I believe he reaches, not only in spite of all man may do, but even using man's evil to further his own plan."[12] Even though we often fail to obey, we must understand that God allows the consequences to teach us to do better in the future. God's will cannot be defeated because God made us for his own purpose. Adam and Eve were deceived by the enemy, who encouraged them to disobey God and become little gods, self-sufficient and self-containing. When Adam and Eve followed Satan's advice, they sinned against God. Sin damaged their relationship with God and one another; it blinded their eyes, warped their thinking, damaged their psyche, sickened their bodies, corrupted their morals, scarred their souls, and shortened their lifespan. They no longer saw life through spiritual lenses; they lost their spiritual sight and connection. They could only see life through their natural eyes and cognition, and we have been seeing and understanding life from our natural senses ever since. Sin has caused humanity to become rebellious, violent, and coldblooded. Scripture states, "Then the Lord saw the wickedness of man was great in the earth, and that every intent of the thoughts of his heart was only evil continually. And the Lord was sorry that He had made man on the earth and He was grieved in His heart" (Gen 6:5–6).

Why was God sorry? Mankind disappointed him. We have chosen to follow our own hearts, evil thoughts, twisted minds, and do the things that seem right in our own eyes. Without God's Spirit and guidance, mankind is nothing more than a destructive force in the world. But,

12. Weatherhead, *The Will of God*, 37.

Created for a Great Purpose

due to God's ultimate will, God decided not to destroy us, but to make a way for us to repent and receive the blessing of eternal life through Jesus Christ. Even though we were tricked by Satan, God's ultimate will is not to be defeated. God made us to be in perpetual relationship with him forever. We have a purpose and the great deceiver cannot thwart the purpose of which God created us. Rick Warren writes, "The purpose of your life is far greater than your own personal fulfillment, your peace of mind, or even your happiness. It's far greater than your family, your career or even your wildest dreams and ambitions. If you want to know why you were placed on this planet, you must begin with God. You were born by His purpose and for His purpose."[13] The way has been made through Jesus Christ for us to be reconciled to God. Life or death—the choice is ours to make. The same decision before Adam and Eve and the children of Israel is also before us today. God says, "I set before you life and death, blessing and cursing; therefore choose life, that you and your descendants may live" (Deut 30:19).

To make the right decision we must be careful whose voice we are listening to. To have a blessed, peaceful, fruitful, and victorious life, we must avoid the counsel of the ungodly. Adam and Eve lost their paradise because they listened to ungodly counsel. The children of Israel wandered in the wilderness for forty years because they listened to ungodly counsel. Samson lost his strength because he listened to ungodly counsel. Saul lost his crown because he listened to ungodly counsel. Judas lost his life because he listened to ungodly counsel. Many lives are

---

13. Warren, *The Purpose Driven Life*, 17.

ruined today; many nations have been brought low, and many leaders have been ruined because they listened to ungodly counsel. When God becomes irrelevant in the decision-making process of a nation, the nation is listening to ungodly counsel. Scripture says, "Blessed is the man [woman, child, and nation] who walks not in the counsel of the ungodly" (Ps 1:1). We must be careful who counsels us, who advises us, and who influences us because the counsel of the ungodly can lead to death, hell, and destruction. We should never walk in the counsel of those who rebel against God and who follow their own way, after their own intelligence, and after their own wisdom. We should never walk in the counsel of the atheist or the humanist, who don't believe God exists and that there are no absolute values, no overruling moral purpose in the universe. We must take care what counsel we heed because "There is a way that seems right to a man, but its end is the way of death" (Prov 14:12). Without God, we would eventually destroy ourselves because we think our way is right; when this happens conflict and death ensue. We must look to God to be able to live out our purpose in life.

Despite the confusion, conflict, war and bloodshed in the world, there is a purpose for our lives. Jesus makes it clear what our purpose is. We must go into all the world and proclaim the good news of the gospel to every creature. Proclaiming the good news is the responsibility of every born-again Christian to help restore the government of God on earth. The good news is the kingdom of God is coming—but not yet. Every nation needs to know that "God so loved the world that he gave his only begotten Son, that whosoever believes in him should not perish but have everlasting life" (John 3:15). How do we live out this love of God? We live it by letting "Our light shine before [the world], that they may see [our] good works and glorify [our] Father in heaven" (Matt 5:16). Our light means that we walk differently; we talk differently, and live differently from the world. Our values, standards, and lifestyles should set us apart from the world. The life we live in Christ is not boring, uninspiring, and unfulfilling. It is just the opposite: exciting, inspiring, and fulfilling. It may seem strange and peculiar to the world because it is. In Christ, we are not only new creatures but also a "chosen generation, a royal priesthood, a holy nation, His own special people, that [we] may proclaim the praises of Him who called [us] out of darkness into his marvelous light" (1 Pet 2:9).

Why are we different? We have been infused by the Spirit of God through Christ. This Spirit has opened up our blinded eyes to see the purpose of God and how we fit into this purpose. Only when the Spirit of God through Christ is infused in us can we see what God has done for us and how we have become new creatures in Christ. Our purpose is to join God through Christ. As God was in Christ reconciling the world unto Himself, we too have been called into this process of reconciling the world unto God through Jesus Christ. When we join Christ in this process and stick with it through all the vicissitudes of life, we can say as Jesus Christ, "I have glorified You on the earth. I have finished the work which You have given me to do" (John 17:4). What a great purpose! What a privilege and awesome responsibility to join Christ to glorify God by carrying out the work God has assigned us to do. The freedom we have obtained through Jesus Christ ought to be lived out to glory God. We were made for a great purpose and this purpose has always been linked to God. The prophet of old spoke about our purpose on earth when he said, "He has shown you, O man, what is good; And what does the Lord require of you but to do justly, love mercy, and walk humbly with your God" (Mic 6:8). Think what our nation and our world would look like if our country and our world sought justice, loved mercy, and walked humbly with God. Until we understand and practice what our purpose on earth is, our nation will continue on its self-destructive course. I hope America's obituary won't read, "The mighty has fallen." They had power without purpose, might without morality, and strength without sight. We must make a choice now between opportunity and obituary. James Russell Lowell wrote,

> Once to every man and nation,
> Comes the moment to decide
> In the strife of truth and falsehood
> For the good or evil side;
> Some great cause God's new Messiah
> Offering each the gloom or blight
> And the choice goes by forever
> Twist that darkness and that light.[14]

While thinking about this decision, let us remember that indecision is not optional. Joshua spoke to the children of Israel "Choose for yourselves this day whom you will serve. . . . But as for me and my house, we will serve the Lord" (Josh 25:15). The prophet Elijah said to the people, "How long will you falter between two opin-

---

14. James Russell Lowell, "The Present Crisis" *Religion in America*, George C. Bedell, Leo Sandon, Charles T. Wellborn, Second Edition, New York: Macmillan Publishing Co., Inc. 1982, 406.

Created for a Great Purpose

ions? If the Lord is God, follow him; but if Baal, follow him" (1 Kgs 18:21). America must make a decision about God because "We cannot serve two masters" (Matt 6:24). We cannot follow Christ and culture. We are created for a great purpose and once we understand and accept this purpose, our lives and nation cannot remain the same. To understand our great purpose, we must begin with God. Without God our existence is meaningless. Without God life and purpose make no sense.

TWO

Freedom without Responsibility

"We shall discover that we always find ourselves caught between our responsibility as citizens of the earth and our responsibility as citizens of heaven."

—Erwin W. Lutzer

One of the greatest endowments given to us by God is freedom. Freedom is a precious, divine gift. To enjoy this precious, divine gift to the fullest, freedom and responsibility must go hand in hand. The two must never be mutually exclusive; and when they are exclusive of one another, chaos and destruction are the result. Freedom does not mean unchecked democracy. It does not mean the absence of moral responsibility. It does not mean unrestrained passions and desires to act as we wish. When we act as we wish without restraint, we create the opposite of what true freedom is: enslavement. We can become enslaved to our own passions, greed, and desires. Yes, God made us free, but we have freedom within boundaries, which are in place to secure—not destroy—our freedom.

Freedom without Responsibility

> We must learn that freedom is not the absence of law, work or labor, but the embracing of responsibility. We must be awakened to the reality that true freedom imposes more laws than slavery, demands more work than slavery and demands more self-control and discipline than slavery. The foundation of true freedom is management—self-management and management of our environment. . . . Therefore, freedom is a return to the responsibility of stewardship.[1]

To have true freedom we must exercise our gifts within the realm of responsibility and within moral laws so we can avoid destroying ourselves and those who share this freedom with us.

Moreover, freedom requires shared responsibility and obedience to moral laws so we won't superimpose our will and way on others. When we superimpose our will and way on others, we create oppression. We must give others the right to exercise their gifts to fulfill their God-given purpose. When we mishandle our freedom and ignore moral laws, we destroy our freedom and create division, strife, and suspension. Was not American slavery an example of irresponsible freedom? Was not our latest financial meltdown in September 2008 an example of irresponsible freedom? Did not Wall Street's irresponsible actions lead to the present housing crisis in which millions lost their homes? Irresponsible action within freedom does affect others. What Wall Street did in private affected the whole economy. We cannot have true freedom when the rich gamble in private and lose and the non-rich have to pay for it. Where is the justice and

1. Munroe, *The Burden of Freedom*, 9.

fairness in this equation? When we are not responsible with our freedom and resources, we cause immeasurable misery for years to come. It is unsettling that those who were responsible for the economic mess in America were rewarded and not held accountable by the government. Myles Monroe made a wise statement, "If you support and finance a mis-manager, you will become complicit in his foolishness and can become part of his mismanagement sin."[2] When the government bails out Wall Street, big banks, and other industries due to mismanagement, the government is complicit in the sin of the mismanagers, which affects the rest of the nation. The freedoms we have in our nation demand responsibility. Without responsibility and accountability, we destroy our nation and its economy. We stand to jeopardize our free enterprise system and everything our nation was founded upon. Just because people are rich doesn't give them the right to jeopardize the rest of the nation. Henry Nelson Wieman makes a very cogent argument of which the wealthiest among us would be wise to listen and practice.

> The wealth of the wealthiest in the economy . . . is sustained and increased by continually increasing the wealth of all. Mass production and automation cannot operate effectively unless all the people have increasing ability to purchase what is produced. These forms of production require great concentration of wealth controlled by a few but at the same time a very great distribution of wealth in the hands of many. Not only must there be a wide distribution of material wealth but also a wide distribution of education and cultural privilege because otherwise the

2. Ibid., 90.

Freedom without Responsibility

many highly equipped minds needed to operate industry will not be available. Also without education and culture, abundant consumption will become destructive.[3]

Walter Rauschenbusch, a social gospel proponent made a similar argument stating that it is our responsibility to remake our present economic system to be fairer and more just to promote brotherly relationship between groups and classes:

> Our business is to make over an antiquated and immoral economic system: to get rid of laws, customs, maxims, and philosophies inherited from an evil and despotic past; to create just and brotherly relations between great groups and classes of society; and thus to lay a social foundation on which modern men individually can live and work in a fashion that will not outrage all the better elements in them.[4]

Everyone, whether wealthy or poor, needs to practice responsibility. Mismanagement among the poor keeps them poor; no matter how much is given to them, they will remain in poverty until they learn to practice sound stewardship principles. Living within our means is wisdom; it helps to stay afloat on the volatile waters of an unpredictable economy. Unlike the rich, when the poor act irresponsibly, they are not rewarded. They are not given a second chance. As unfair as this may be, the reality is the poor must be good stewards of what they have. Just because people are poor doesn't mean they have to be poor

---

3. Wieman, *Creative Freedom,* 100–101.

4. Walter Rauschenbusch, *Religion in America*, Second Edition, 341.

managers or have poor relationships, discipline, morals, minds, grades, attitudes, and expectations. Responsibility ought to be a principle that all people practice, regardless of race, class, and socio-economic standing. Unless we are careful how we exercise our freedom, entrapments of every kind will have a firm hold on us. Irresponsible freedom can carry us back to those bygone days of the Great Depression and social unrest. We must learn the lessons of the past and understand that "It is for freedom that Christ has set us free. Stand firm, then, and do not let yourselves be burdened again by the yoke of slavery" (Gal 5:1). Irresponsible freedom can easily repeat history. The spirit of sin and oppression has been broken by Jesus Christ, and to take this for granted and live irresponsibly is foolish. Irresponsible living is detrimental not only to oneself but also to the whole nation.

When God led the children of Israel out of bondage, they acted irresponsibly with their freedom. They complained about what they were missing in Egypt, rebelled against authority, became lawless, and did not trust nor appreciate the freedom and resources God had given them. Their misuse of freedom led them to commit idolatry. They wasted their gold, made a golden calf, and gave credit to it for leading them out of bondage. Their reckless behavior caused them not to inherit the Promised Land. Therefore, they wandered in the wilderness forty years and perished. God took the next generation to the Promised Land. God will not reward recklessness, irresponsibility, and stubborn hearts and minds with blessings. Until people and nations are willing to be transformed by the renewing of their minds, they will never receive God's promises. We must learn

Freedom without Responsibility

and practice responsibility because our future and the future of our children and grandchildren depend upon it. Responsibility is foundational for enjoying true freedom. When we allow recklessness to replace responsibility in the name of freedom, as a nation we have given ourselves over to pestilence and decay.

Would you give an irresponsible son or daughter access to your bank account? Would you allow a reckless friend to drive your car when he or she has several DUIs? Would you trust your child with a known pedophile? Would you continue to elect to office leaders who are irresponsible with your tax money? The answer to these questions is a resounding "*no*" because each of these situations shows recklessness and irresponsible behavior. So it is with God toward us. God will not give us more or take us higher in life when we are irresponsible and disregard moral laws. It doesn't matter the number of messages we hear about this being your season to be blessed; God is about to take you to greater heights. Understand, there can be no advancement and promotion in our lives or in the life of our nation until we get back to being responsible and respecting morality. Both Wall Street and Main Street must realize this truth. Don't be fooled into thinking we can receive greater blessings and higher promotions when we act irresponsibly. False promotions may come but never from God. When they come from other than God, they are curses covered with attractive packaging.

For example, in (Matt 4:2-9) the devil offers Jesus the kingdoms of the world and the glory of them; this was a promotion teaser, a curse wrapped in beautiful packaging. There is a string attached to this false blessing: Jesus must worship the devil. Anything you worship you will obey; you will show loyalty. Therefore, we must be careful about doing wrong and receiving promotions for it. This is nothing but a trick from the enemy to keep you engaged in doing wrong until you and everything around you are destroyed. Doing what is right and being responsible may take time for a promotion, but when God blesses, he adds no sorrow with it (Prov 10:22). When blessings come from God they are sure and secure. It is better to practice responsibility and morality and have favor with God than to act irresponsibly and rewarded for it by the world. We must beware who rewards us. When irresponsible behavior is rewarded (by the government, by parents, etc.) the wellbeing of the nation is jeopardized. It threatens freedom and democracy to the point that America borrows money from other nations like China to run the country. We must remember (Prov 22:7): "The borrower is the servant or slave to the lender?" We cannot maintain freedom and democracy borrowing from other nations just to function. Thomas Jefferson understood that the accumulation of enormous debt is not only irresponsible but also dangerous to the nation. He said,

> I place economy among the first and most important virtues, and public debt as the greatest of dangers. To preserve our independence, we must not let our rulers load us with perpetual debt .... The principle of spending money to be paid by future generations, under the name of funding, is but swindling futurity on a large scale .... I predict future happiness for Americans if they can prevent the government from wasting

Freedom without Responsibility

> the labors of the people under the pretense of taking care of them.[5]

The American people must hold accountable those who govern them. Who stands to lose when the government acts irresponsibly? The people do. Who stands to lose when the custodians of our economy acts irresponsibly? The people do. We must understand that "Irresponsibility is freedom's deadliest enemy."[6] When we are irresponsible we stand to lose whatever we have. We could lose our marriage, children, house, reputation, savings, and nation. When we lose our values, we lose our moral obligations; when we lose our moral obligations, we lose our nation; when we lose our economy, we lose our sovereignty. Once we lose our sovereignty, it is hard if not impossible to regain it. America is losing its sovereignty in leading the world in democracy. Unless the American people hold accountable the mismanagers on Wall Street and in the government, America will continue to lose its respected place in the world.

The generation of the children of Israel that marched out of Egypt lost their approval to go into the Promised Land because they were irresponsible and mismanaged the freedom God had given them. As Myles Monroe has written,

> Whatever [we] mismanage [we] will lose.. When Adam mismanaged his job assignment in the Garden, he not only lost his job—he also lost his home. He was kicked out of the Garden. To

---

5. Thomas Jefferson Quotes from Working Minds, Issue #54, #59, ibid, blog 10/2007., G.E. Nordell, "Working Minds Philosophy of Empowerment" Issue #72.

6. Monroe, *The Burden of Freedom*, 66.

> whom did God give the Garden? He gave it to man. Who took the Garden from man? God did. Who put him out? God did.. The devil didn't put Adam out of the Garden–God did.[7]

When we are irresponsible and mismanage what God has given us, it will be taken away because responsibility and good management are inseparable. Being responsible with what God has given us will determine how long we keep the blessings we have. There is an adage that says, "When we waste money, one day we will wish we had it. If we lose our reputation, one day we will wish we had it." Irresponsibility only brings about want and sorrow later.

Tap any person on the shoulder who has lost something of great value due to being irresponsible and they will tell you that if they could do it over they would be more conscientious and responsible. Ask people who have lost their health due to irresponsible living, and they will tell you that if they could go back and relive their lives, they would choose the path of responsibility. Ask any young woman who was sexually irresponsible and lost her innocence; she will tell you that if she could do it over again, she would choose a different path. Ask any young man who became irresponsible because he wanted quick cash and committed a crime and ended up in prison; he will tell you if he could go back and change his decision, he would make a different decision. Ask any irresponsible student who was on a scholarship but lost it will tell you if he or she could go back in time, the decision to act responsibly would be the choice. There is a price to pay

---

7. Ibid., 91–92.

Freedom without Responsibility

when we are irresponsible with our freedom. We cannot change our irresponsible past but we can start living a responsible present, which will bless us in the future. The decision we make in the present affects our future. This is why Paul Tillich said this about the present:

> The present is the future. To live in the present is to live in tension toward the future; every present is essentially a transition out of the past into the future. Spirit or mind is always direction from that which is to that which ought to be. To understand the present means to see its inner tension toward the future. In this field also there is such a thing as spiritual perspective, the possibility of finding amid all the infinite aspirations and tensions which every present contains not only those which conserve the past but also those which are creatively new and pregnant with the future. . . . To understand the present means ultimately to understand the future with which the womb of the present is great. But if spirit is direction, tension toward the future, then every outlook toward the future from the point of view of the present is also necessarily directed and tense, in short, the outlook of a creative will, not merely of indifferent observation.[8]

Therefore, we must be careful how we practice our present freedom. The freedom we enjoy today demands responsibility and obedience so we won't slip into entrapping situations in the future. We must have moral laws to live out true freedom. When we violate natural, moral and spiritual laws, we undermine our freedom. For example, speed limits are posted not to inhibit our freedom of driving but to enhance it. But when drivers ignore

8. Tillich, *The Religious Situation*, 33–34.

speed limits on a crowded highway, the freedom of the other drivers is thrown into jeopardy. Likewise, when we practice freedom without responsibility, we endanger not only our lives but also the lives of our family, community, and nation. Recklessness can only lead to death. When we look at America and see recklessness from the top down, we are in the process of changing our national anthem from "The land of the free and the home of the brave" to "The death of democracy and the home of the irresponsible." It would be an anthem of sorrow.

It is a shame that our national debt has spiraled out of control. This threatens our national security. Instead of Washington, DC practicing a culture of cooperation to steer our great country back to responsibility, it has become a culture of competition and destruction. Politicians on both sides refuse to put patriotism and people before profit, and we are worse off because of it. How can America point the way of democracy in the world when it has put at peril its own freedoms? What has happen to a government of the people, by the people, and for the people? Until our leaders understand that a nation divided cannot stand, our liberties will become our liabilities. By this I mean when people's liberties clash with one another and everybody is doing what they want without restraint and responsibility, liberties have become liabilities. Until our nation gets back to moral and fiscal responsibility we minimize our liberties and maximize our liabilities.

Some people may argue that faith and patriotism should be mutually exclusive as they argue for the separation of state and religion. But, when the nation is morally declining, those who are of the Christian faith should point the way to a nobler path. Love of country and faith

Freedom without Responsibility

must go hand and hand. Faith is not the enemy of patriotism. William Wilberforce said,

> If patriotism is defined in such a way that it is really nationalism—that is, the use of all available power and resources to impose the will of one nation on another—then surely authentic faith is the enemy. But if patriotism is a love for one's country and the desire to see justice, peace and good will toward all men prevail, then faith is not the enemy but the best friend of such patriotism. . . . It would be like saying that the principle of gravity is limiting to human freedom without recognizing the role it plays in keeping the universe intact.[9]

The Christian involvement in the direction of the nation is not only a Christian duty but also a moral responsibility as a citizen. It doesn't matter what political party is in power,

> [t]he Christian has to be concerned with "moving" society in a much deeper and more positive sense . . . the aim will be to create a society in which the weak are protected, the casualties are cared for, everyone has some say in what happens to [them], no one is denied justice or the necessities of life, and everyone feels that he has the opportunity to contribute.[10]

The Apostle Paul helps us to understand the purpose of liberty. Liberty is not unchecked freedom. Paul says that this liberty we have been called to is an opportunity for us to serve one another through love. God called Americans to liberty to serve one another and others through love.

9. Wilberforce, *Real Christianity*, 151.
10. Hinchliff, *Holiness and Politics*, 185.

God didn't call Americans to oppress, exploit, and destroy one another. This call to liberty was not to fulfill greed for power to indulge in irresponsible behavior. We have been called to liberty to fulfill a purpose, and this purpose is to do the will of God on earth. The liberty we have been called to is not cheap liberty. God paid the full price for our liberty. He bought our liberty through the death of his only begotten Son, and "Whosoever believes in him shall not perish but have everlasting life" (John 3:16). So, don't think this liberty we have been called to in Christ Jesus is cheap. Don't think this liberty in America is cheap. Many men and women over the course of our national history paid the price for our liberty. Our national graveyards are full of soldiers who lost their lives for our liberty. The price others paid for our liberty ought to be appreciated, respected, and honored. The liberty people have died for should motivate us to practice freedom responsibly as one way to honor them for the great sacrifice they have made on our behalf. It is the height of irresponsibility to mismanage liberty when God's Son and so many more have given up their lives for us to enjoy it. We must recapture the spirit of gratitude within our practice of liberty.

Paul tells us that we "have been called to liberty; only do not use liberty for as an opportunity for the flesh, but through love serve one another" (Gal 5:13). Liberty has a divine, social, and economic purpose. The divine purpose for liberty is to show the world what God has done through Christ to redeem us and set us free: "And that they may come to their senses and escape the snare of the devil, having been taken captive by him to do his will" (2 Tim 2:26). Through the death of Jesus Christ, God has purchased us to do his will. Once we fulfill God's purpose

Freedom without Responsibility

of liberty we can then fulfill the social purpose of liberty, which is to serve one another through love. This means taking care of our families, looking out for our neighbors, enjoying and encouraging our friends, sharing time and resources with those who are less fortunate, and cooperating with and holding accountable those who have authority over us. This produces a healthy and godly nation. When we have a healthy and godly nation, we can achieve the economic purpose of liberty, and that is to have jobs and services available so everyone can work and pay their fair share to run the country responsibly. This is responsible democracy. As Christopher Lasch has written,

> Democracy works best when men and women do things for themselves, with the help of their friends and neighbors, instead of depending on the state. Not that democracy should be equated with rugged individualism. Self-reliance does not mean self-sufficiency. Self-governing communities, not individuals, are the basic unit of democratic society . . . it is the decline of those communities, more than anything else, that calls the future of democracy into question.[11]

Making sure everyone contributes in one way or another their God given gifts and talents to help keep the nation morally strong and responsible is democracy. Liberty doesn't mean take necessities of the many to provide luxuries for the few. It doesn't mean wiping out the middle class by unfair taxing. It doesn't mean the top two percent live in opulence and ninety-eight percent are struggling to make ends meet. Thomas Paine reminds us in "Common Sense" that

11. Lasch, *The Revolt of the Elites*, 7–8.

> It is inhumane to talk of a million sterling a year, paid out of the public taxes of any country for the support of any individual, whilst thousands who are forced to contribute thereto, are pining with want, and struggling with misery. Government does not consist in a contrast between prisons and palaces, between poverty and pomp; it is not instituted to rob the needy of his mite, and increase the wretchedness of the wretched.[12]

"Liberty" doesn't mean this country becomes an entitlement state in which people depend on the government to take care of them. A *hand up* to assist people to get on their feet is a moral responsibility. A *handout* in which people depend on the government to do for them what they can do for themselves is morally irresponsible. Resources will eventually run out when we have a situation of outgoing handouts but no incoming revenue to pay for it. It is like a withdrawal and deposit situation. If we constantly withdraw and make no deposits, the account will be depleted. Liberty means helping to create a society where people live responsibly and having a system of checks and balances to maintain a strong and vibrant nation.

There is no other nation that equals America in freedom. People around the world want to come to America to enjoy the freedom and opportunities that are available here like nowhere else. America has been the symbol of liberty and has carried the torch of freedom and democracy around the world. We pride ourselves on our liberty. We have laws protecting our liberty. Our legal system, while not perfect, is designed to protect our liberties.

---

12. Paine, *Common Sense and Other Writings*, 225.

Freedom without Responsibility

We are a free nation like no other on the earth. We don't have to worry about being harassed, arrested, and put in jail for thinking what we want, believing what we want, achieving what we want, working where we want and living where we want. These liberties come with our citizenship, and we should not take these liberties for granted. God through Christ has called Americans to liberty, and this is why "We pledge our allegiance to the flag of the United States of America; And to the Republic for which it stands, one nation under God indivisible with liberty and justice for all." God has called Americans to liberty.

But, instead of using this liberty to serve people through love, Americans are using this liberty as an opportunity to get all they can no matter how they get it. The end justifies the means. William Wilberforce made a very insightful statement:

> That which is intended to motivate goodness and restrain evil actually can become the instrument of that which it intended to restrain. History is full of examples of how virtues such as liberty or patriotism become twisted when separated from a healthy and authentic faith. Twisted men in every generation and occupation have twisted whatever they must twist to get what they want.[13]

America cannot remain a free and democratic nation as long as the rich are getting richer and the poor are getting poorer; as long as jobs are outsourced to other countries; as long as people are thrown out of their homes because their jobs have been eliminated and banks refuse to work with them; as long as outrageous prices for basic

13. Wilberforce, *Real Christianity*, 46.

healthcare are constantly rising; and as long as God is being pushed out of the social and economic order. It is inevitable that when God is pushed out of our nation it is on the verge of social and economic collapse. Corruption, greed, and irresponsible management must be eliminated from our body politic. We can no longer afford to be silent and indifferent onlookers. Christopher Lasch reminds us:

> In our time democracy is more seriously threatened by indifference than by intolerance or superstition. We have become too proficient in making excuses for ourselves—worse, in making excuses for the "disadvantaged." We are so busy defending our rights (rights conferred, for the most part, by judicial decree) that we give little thought to our responsibilities. We seldom say what we think, for fear of giving offense. We are determined to respect everyone, but we have forgotten that respect has to be earned. Respect is not another word for tolerance or the appreciation of "alternative lifestyles and communities." This is a tourist's approach to morality. Respect is what we experience in the presence of admirable achievement, admirably formed characters, natural gifts put to good use. It entails the exercise of discriminating judgment, not indiscriminate acceptance.[14]

Warning! If America is unwilling to reform from within, our national downfall won't come from without. Martin Luther King, Jr. understood that unless America is willing to reform, she may be counted among the nations that fell. He said,

---

14. Lasch, *The Revolt of the Elites and the Betrayal of Democracy*, 89.

Freedom without Responsibility

> Arnold Toynbee has said that some twenty-six civilizations have risen upon the face of the earth. Almost all of them have descended into the junk heaps of destruction. The decline and fall of these civilizations, according to Toynbee, was not caused by external invasions but by internal decay. They failed to respond creatively to the challenges impinging upon them. If western civilization does not now respond constructively . . . some future historian will have to say that a great civilization died because it lacked the soul and commitment to make justice a reality for all [people].[15]

The choice is ours to change our present course.

Unless we inject again moral responsibility in the veins of our nation, the autopsy will read "national suicide." It is not known if our national death will come with a bang or a whimper, but we can be assured unless we change our reckless behavior, it will surely come. The economic crisis of 2008–2009 that put this nation at the financial cliff was strictly due to irresponsible behavior. We must reform or fall. Jim Wallis advises, "If our goal is to get back to business as usual, we will soon be right back to what got us into so much trouble, because what was usual is exactly what got us here in the first place. To go back to business as usual would be to miss the opportunity this crisis provided to change our ways and return to some of our oldest and best values."[16]

Americans who say that national collapse can't happen here should reflect on history and see all those nations that fell who didn't believe it could happen. It happened

---

15. King, Jr., Where Do We Go from Here?" 623.
16. Wallis, *Rediscovering Values*, 5.

to Britain in the 1940s and other places. America is not immune from economic takeover. Phillips explains,

> In light of the trends in manufacturing and the credit markets alike, there is little doubt left about the next dominant continent, Asia, and the next leading world economic power—China, possibly in the 2030's, barring some extraordinary disruption. This prospect, coupled with China's emergent role as a leading U.S. Creditor, is part of what has to warn Americans, just as the surging economic growth of both the United States and Germany became a warning to Britain in the 1890s.[17]

In the quest to have rights in America we must never forget the wisdom of the ages which says, "Let us hear the conclusion of the whole matter: Fear God and keep his commandments for this is the whole duty of [humanity]" (Eccl 12:13).

---

17. Phillips, *American Theocracy*, 378.

THREE

The Enemy Who Deceives Us

"Be sober; be vigilant; because your adversary the devil walks about like a roaring lion, seeking whom he may devour. Resist him, steadfast in the faith, knowing that the same sufferings are experienced by your brotherhood in the world." (1 Pet 5:8–9, NKJV)

There is something sinister going on in our nation and social institutions. There is a spirit of meanness, disrespect, and evil being played out before our eyes. It is not just in the government, prisons, schools, colleges and universities; we see it also in families and in the postmodern church. Martin Luther King Jr. wrote,

> Within the wide arena of everyday life we see evil in all of its ugly dimensions. We see it expressed in tragic lust and inordinate selfishness. We see it in high places where [people] are willing to sacrifice truth on the altars of their self-interest. We see it in imperialistic nations crushing other people with the battering rams of social injustice. We see it clothed in the garments of calamitous wars which leave

[people] and nations morally and physically bankrupt.[1]

We may have heard clichés such as, *The devil is busy; the devil made me do it; that's nothing but the devil; the devil is in him; speaking of the devil;* and *here comes the devil.* These clichés are repeated again and again. Very few people understand the personality that has thrown the whole world in turmoil. If there is not an adequate understanding of this malevolent personality in our midst, we will continue to be his victims.

Whether we know it or not, Satan is the prince of this world. The systems and institutions of this world have been designed and implemented by the devil to produce oppression, poverty, homelessness, and other systemic problems that crush the people of God. We must see the devil in a much broader sense than the limited traditional views of him. To understand evil and its ugly manifestations, we have to trace the cause of it. Just as when we have certain symptoms, the doctor traces the cause of these symptoms to understand their origin to prescribe a cure. The day the first humans decided to disobey God, the world became a constant turmoil of suffering. Hatred, war, bloodshed, discord, and death have been humans' constant companions. Suffering, violence, and death have become so common place in the world many people cannot believe there is a loving God. They cannot reconcile an all-powerful God with the problem of evil. They don't understand that behind every effect is a cause.

What caused human alienation from God and the subsequent suffering of human beings? Who is behind it?

1. King, Jr., *Strength to Love*, 76–77.

The Enemy Who Deceives Us

The cause behind human misery is Satan, who is known as "An adversary, the accuser, the deceiver, the evil one, the destroyer," and the incorrigible fallen archangel who became the devil. Jesus called him "the father of lies" (John 8:44). Satan, the devil, deceived humans because God replaced Satan and the fallen angels with humans who would govern the earth. Humans were created to carry out what the angels failed to do: "This earth, originally, was intended to be the abode of a third of all the angels. The angels, beholding the earth at its creation, found it so beautiful and perfect they shouted spontaneously for joy" (Job 38:4–7). It was to provide a glorious opportunity for them. They were to work the land, produce from it, and preserve and increase its beauty.[2]

God created the earth and the universe, and the angels were supposed to be good stewards over God's creation. The chief archangel God put in charge was Lucifer. He was anointed with beauty, power, intelligence, authority, and wisdom. His dazzling appeal of sardius, topaz, diamond, beryl, onyx, jasper, sapphire, turquoise, and emerald with gold was so magnificent that his dealing place was on the mountain of God; and he walked among fiery stones (Ezek 28:13–14). God put every gem of precious stone on him to wear and distinguished him from the rest of the angels. God set him as the top seraphim over many other angels, and his throne was on the earth. Lucifer was supposed to lead the other angels in carrying out the will of God on earth. But, we find in Ezekiel 28:15 that Lucifer was "Perfect until iniquity was found in him." How could sin enter such a perfect being? God did not

2. Armstrong, *The Incredible Human Potential*, 52.

create sin. God created free will in angels and humans alike, knowing very well that this free will means the possibility of rebellion. God could have made robots out of both angels and humans, but robots are programmed and have no power to reason, decide, or challenge their creator. Furthermore, robots can neither love nor respond to love. They do not have the capacity to feel. Since God is love, God chose not to create beings without the capacity to feel, love, and respond to love.

Lucifer, who was created with perfection and free will, became prideful and ignored the God who created him. By his own free will, Lucifer turned to lawlessness. He desired to have his throne above the Most High God, and he deceived a third of the angels with him; they formed an unholy alliance to dethroned God. Herbert W. Armstrong wrote, "He became jealous of God, envious, and resentful of God. He allowed lust and greed to fill him, and he became bitter. This inspired a spirit of violence! He deliberately became his Maker's adversary and enemy. That was his choice, not God's—yet allowed by God!"[3] R. T. Kendall makes a similar argument that it was outright jealousy that caused Lucifer to rebel against his Creator.

> It was jealousy that lay behind Satan's decision to revolt. The prophet Isaiah was given a glimpse as to what happened. Called "morning star"—"Lucifer, son of the morning" (Isa 14:12)—Satan fell from heaven after jealousy took over. Satan said, "I will ascend to heaven; I will raise my throne above the stars of God; I will sit enthroned on the mount of assembly, on

3. Ibid., 54.

the utmost heights of the sacred mountain. I will
make myself like the Most High" (Isa 14:12–14).
... In a word: Satan was jealous of God."[4]

When jealousy has taken root in the heart, Kendall warns us: "Jealousy can lead us to do crazy things, like losing one's own soul."[5]

The rebellion against God was put down, and the angels were punished for their sin. In (2 Peter 2:4) it says "For if God did not spare the angels who sinned, but cast them down into hell and delivered them into chains of darkness, to be reserved for judgment" humans will receive the same judgment if they follow the path of the deceiver. Again, God did not create Satan; Lucifer became Satan when he freely chose to go against his Creator. It is not known how long it took Lucifer to convince a third of the angels to follow him in this plot. It may have taken billions of years before his plan was revealed. We must remember that all of this was pre-human history. It transpired before God created humans. The archangel Lucifer refused to establish the government of God on earth and was therefore fired and thrown from his appointed place. Although he was created wise, charismatic, and endowed with beauty and persuasion, his sin was mutiny. He gambled and lost! The angels who threw their lot in with him also lost and were punished by God. Knowing that they can no longer live with God now or in the future, Satan and his demons want to deceive the world in following him toward his final destruction. Just like he led a third of the angels against God, Satan is trying to lead human-

---

4. Kendall, *Jealousy: The Sin No One Talks About*, 32–33.

5. Ibid., 49.

ity in rebellion against God, and he is doing a very good job achieving it. But, he won't be any more successful this time than he was in the beginning.

Scripture points out that when Lucifer was thrown out of heaven there was a loud voice that said, "Woe to the inhabitants of the earth and the sea (Rev 12:12). Satan is full of wrath and bitterness and deceives the nations because he knows he has a short time before God destroys him. Satan is busy trying to get every human soul to come under this same death sentence. Humans must be on the alert at all times because, as Peter pointed out, "Your adversary the devil walks about like a roaring lion, seeking whom he may devour" (1 Pet 5:8). Satan is roaming the earth to devour the unsuspecting, the unbelieving, the ignorant, and the fearful. One only needs to observe the national and international scene to know that Satan is at work deceiving and manipulating nations to rise up against one another. All the bloodshed, confusion, strife, and discord in the world are the influence of Satan. All the gun violence and senseless deaths we see at home and abroad is instigated by Satan. As Hal Lindsey writes,

> Behind all that is tangible in the world system there is the intangible genius of Satan, the master deceiver. Behind "the things of the world system" is the mastermind who uses them to shift our focus from devotion to Christ to devotion to things. Once this is done the inevitable ever-increasing force of greed sets in.[6]

Paul tells us to "Put on the whole armor of God that you may be able to stand against the wiles of the devil.

---

6. Lindsey, *Satan Is Alive and Well on Planet Earth*, 77.

The Enemy Who Deceives Us

For we do not wrestle against flesh and blood, but against principalities, against powers, against the rulers of the darkness of this age, against spiritual hosts of wickedness in the heavenly places" (Eph 6:11–12).

If only Americans could understand that our struggle has never been racial, but spiritual wickedness. Satan and his demons are the real cause behind racial hostility, social inequality, and class warfare. Satan has entered the minds of people who have misinterpreted and distorted the Bible. For example in (Gen 9:24–26), Noah cursed his younger son and said he would be a servant to his brethren Shem and Japheth. Oppressors took this scripture to justify American slavery. It was a misinterpretation of the text but nevertheless it set in motion pseudoscience and bad theology based upon skin color to arouse animosity, hatred, and discord. Satan wants to keep humans fighting and killing each other. Hal Lindsey states,

> In this role Satan injects his treachery into the educational system, the philosophy, the mass media, the arts, the style, and the culture. He will use a lake of truth to disguise a pint of poison. His deceptions about life and its purpose are lethal. Any flirting with the ways of the world can lead to spiritual adultery (James 4:4).[7]

Satan is so cunning that he can confuse people to lose their power of objectivity to the point that they call "Evil good, and good evil; put darkness for light, and light for darkness; put bitter for sweet, and sweet for bitter" (Isa 5:20). Behind color prejudice and hatred is the great adversary of God and humans: Satan.

---

7. Ibid., 80.

From Wall Street to Main Street

Unless Americans understand the cause of its racial strife, and the science and philosophy that support it, strife among the races will intensify and bring about the demise of this great republic. God did not make a superior race nor did God make an inferior race. America's past is full of books and literature pointing out the inferiority of blacks and other minorities. All of this is the result of being under the power and delusion of Satan. He wants the races to destroy each other. Satan wants America to destroy itself. At the very root of racial strife, injustice, and inequality is Satan our adversary whose tentacles are in every nation of the world. Robert F. Kennedy stated, "The enemies of a solution to the racial dilemma are not the black man or the white man. The enemies are fear and indifference. They are hatred and above all, letting monetary passion blind us to a clear and reasoned understanding of the realities of the land."[8] The words *fear*, *indifference*, *hatred*, and *blindness* are all traits that come from Satan, who uses these things to accomplish his purpose on the earth, which is "To steal, to kill, and to destroy" (John 10:10). While we are watching out for terrorism at home and abroad, let us not forget the real enemy behind terrorism: Satan.

He poisons the air with anti-American, anti-Muslim, anti-Jewish information, knowledge, and doctrine to lead us into a bloody war. We now have the capacity to wipe out the human race. Satan wants the human race annihilated to grieve the heart of God. Due to Satan's influence on the world, many people have fallen away from the faith. Scripture predicted this would happen:

8. Foluke, *The Real Holocaust*, 392.

The Enemy Who Deceives Us

"Now the Spirit expressly says that in the latter times some will depart from the faith, giving heed to deceiving spirits and doctrines of demons speaking lies in hypocrisy, having their own conscience seared with a hot iron" (1 Tim 4:1-2). So many people have been deceived by the influence of Satan that their consciences have become numb. When people don't live with a conscience, they are dangerous and will do anything. We may ask how some people commit so many inhumane acts on other people, especially children, and are without remorse. People who have not listened to their consciences over time have become numb. These people are menace to society; they are demon-possessed; they are callous and cold with no God consciousness at all.

In every walk of life, Satan and the demons are there to influence us. We see Satan's influence in governments, homes, communities, schools, and the church. There is no human habitation where the tentacles of his influence are not felt. Satan deceives humans into believing that it is God—not Satan—who is their enemy. All the chaos, hatred, wars and bloodshed in the world is not the work of God but the work of the deceiver. As long as humans follow Satan through the flesh instead of God through the Spirit there will always be discord, strife, misery, and death. Whatever God commands humans not to do; Satan influences them to do. He never wants humans to obey God because of the blessings and future inheritance it brings. Therefore, he twists, manipulates, confuses, and deceives humans in every way possible to rebel against God. Herbert W. Armstrong alerts us.

> Grasp It! Satan is here called "the prince of the power of the air"! . . . This great and powerful being, even though evil, has power literally to surcharge the air around this earth. He broadcasts! . . . The spirit in every human being is automatically tuned in on Satan's wavelength. You don't hear anything because he does not broadcast in words—nor in sounds, whether music or otherwise. He broadcasts in Attitudes. He broadcasts in attitudes of self-centeredness, lust, greed, vanity, jealousy, envy, resentment, competition, strife, bitterness and hate.
>
> In a word, the selfishness, hostility, deceitfulness, wickedness, rebellion, etc. that we call "Human Nature" is actually Satan's Nature. It is Satan's attitude. And broadcasting it, surcharging the air with it, Satan actually works in unsuspecting all over the world! That is how Satan deceives the whole world today (Rev 12:9 and 20:3). Being invisible, people do not see or hear him. This prince of the power of the air—this god of this world—is the real source of what we have come to call "Human Nature"! Here is the cause of all the world's evils![9]

When God dethroned Lucifer and placed humans over the created earth, Satan deceived them and the authority God gave to humans were placed in the hand of the deceiver. As a result the world will never be at peace. There will always be strife, war, and death. Satan is going to make sure that no nation will ever live by the principles of the kingdom of God. As long as Satan is the prince of this world, there will always be tension among nations. We cannot literally see Satan and the demons because they are spirits as God is Spirit, but they are diametrically

9. Armstrong, *The Incredible Human Potential*, 146–47.

opposed to God, goodness, justice, and righteousness. No human apparatus can produce a picture of this great deceiver. There have been caricatures of Hollywood of the devil with a crown, red eyes, folk and pointed ears–but this is not a true picture of the great deceiver. If the devil really looked like this, we could easily avoid him.

We must remember that Lucifer, before he turned into Satan, was created with beauty and majesty. So, Satan tempts humans with beautiful sights and the promise of power to lure them into his deceptive ways. Look at how he tempted Jesus: "Again, the devil takes him up into an exceedingly high mountain, and showed him all the kingdoms of the world and their glory; and he said to him, 'All these things I will give you, if you will fall down and worship me'" (Matt 4:8–9). Jesus resisted the devil's temptations, but the devil is not easily discouraged. He may not be successful the first time, but be assured he will return to take another strike at his target. The devil never gives up on getting humans to serve him.

He constantly tempts us because as James P. Gills points out,

> He knows that we are what we think. This battle for our mind is the most important fight of our life because the choices we make, influenced by our thoughts and imaginations, determine our eternal destiny. . . . Satan comes through many conduits and channels. He may be dressed well, culturally accepted and advertised beautifully, but he is still Satan. He will attack each of us differently, because he knows our individual weaknesses. But he seeks the same result in each of us. He wants to blind us to the glory of Christ.[10]

10. Gills, *Imaginations*, 97–98.

Paul tells us that "Satan transforms himself into an angel of light" (2 Cor 11:14). If humans are not careful, things that are pleasing to the natural eye can be the trick of the devil. We must remember that Satan is an expert in allurement. Since he is powerful enough to deceive a third of the angels, he is even more powerful to deceive humans who were made a little lower than the angels (Ps 8:5).

Many people deny the existence of the devil because they cannot literally see him. Just as we cannot see the wind, we know it is a reality. Likewise, Satan is a reality. Milton put it most poetically: "Millions of spiritual creatures walk the earth unseen, both when we wake, and when we sleep."[11] Jesus describes them as walking through "Dry places seeking rest" (Luke 11:24). Demons want to find rest by possessing people's bodies because they don't have physical bodies. Once they are cast out of one person they seek another person or try to repossess the person they were once in by bringing along seven more demons much more wicked than they are. When a young man was possessed with demons, "He was kept under guard, bound with chains and shackles; and he broke the bonds and was driven by the demon into the wilderness. When the young man met Jesus, Jesus asked him, 'What is your name?' And he said, 'Legion,' because many demons had entered him" (Luke 8:29–30). When Jesus ordered these demons out of the young man, they begged to go into the swine. They "entered the swine and the herd ran violently down the steep place into the lake and drowned" (Luke 8:33). Demons are looking to rest

---

11. John Milton, *Paradise Lost*, The Complete English Poems, Edited by Gordon Campbell, 239–40.

The Enemy Who Deceives Us

in people, use people, and ultimately destroy people as they did with the swine. It is extremely important for us to guard against the devil and the demons because they are out to destroy humanity. When we hear of the senseless killings in America and around the world, we know demons have entered people to influence them to destroy other people. We must beware of the devil and demons for they are seeking whom they can destroy. Don't become their victims by ignorance. Armstrong reminds us,

> Satan, prince of the power of the air, stirs the spirits of humans, injecting into them attitudes, moods, and impulses of selfishness, vanity, lust and greed, attitudes of resentment against authority, of jealousy and envy, of competition and strife, of resentment and bitterness, of violence, murder and war. People do not recognize the source of these attitudes, feelings, motives and impulses.... They do not see the invisible Satan. They hear no audible voice. They do not know the attitude came from Satan (Revelation 12:9). That is how Satan deceives the whole world.[12]

Many people just don't believe in nonmaterial beings roaming the earth. They cannot believe that such a host of malevolent forces is operating in the world. It is said that "the greatest trick of the devil is to convince the world he doesn't exist." Satan wants people to believe that he is an illusion, a myth, a metaphysical idea, and a creation of the human mind. He wants scientists and scholars to dismiss him as a superstition, a figment of the imagination, an old wives' tale. It is hard to put up a defense against something people don't believe exists. To dismiss the reality of

---

12. Armstrong, *The Incredible Human Potential*, 147.

the devil is to blame everything wrong, evil, and unjust in the world on God. Many people have become atheists because they cannot fathom the goodness of God in light of an evil world. Not able to understand what is happening in the spirit world, many scientists and scholars just deny it which works to the advantage of the deceiver.

Whether people believe or not doesn't change the fact that the devil is real. Evil is real. Hate is real. Wickedness is real. Murder is real. Injustice is real. The things that divide and separate us from God and ourselves are real. The envy and jealousy among us, the hatred and strife among us, the war and bloodshed among us; and all of the things that make life a nightmare come from one source: the devil. The devil is ever-present, and if we are not careful, he will lure us into his traps. Paul says, "When I would do good, evil is present with me" (Rom 7:21). Wherever there is goodness, peace, and love Satan is present to pervert it and turn it into wickedness to achieve his purpose in the world. To overcome Satan, we must resist his influence because he deceives the whole world.

Unless Americans understand the tricks and trade of the enemy, our country will continue to decline and lose its moral bearings. Regardless of who believes that religion has no place in public life, does not negate the fact that the enemy is chipping away at democracy, justice, and equality to cause the demise of this great republic. When national shame no longer produces moral outrage, the enemy has shot another bullet in the body of democracy. When a nation loves money more than morality, rights more than righteousness, and privileges more than principles, this equals the downfall of the nation. To defeat the genius of deception, the great divider of the human race, and the prince of darkness, we must

> Check out our armor, keeping it polished and oiled at all times, ready for active duty. If our sword is getting rusty because we haven't been studying the Word, we'd better sharpen it. If our breastplate is slipping out of place because we are getting on the performance-kick, we'd better adjust it. If our helmet is off because we are not sure about our salvation, then we'd better get into the Word of God or go to someone who knows the Word. . . . We cannot afford to be tin soldiers: we do not dare play games with Satan. He is capturing [people] right and left, using all his arsenal of weapons to do it.[13]

Like never before we are in a spiritual struggle to save the life and soul of America. There is an African proverb that says, "If we conquer the enemy within the one without can do us no harm." We must conquer our rebellion against God, our demons, our greed, our selfishness, our pride, our arrogance, our superiority complex, and most of all our racial ignorance and hatred of one another. Unless we conquer these things within us, Satan and the demons will make sure that life remains a nightmare and an unending holocaust among the nations of the world.

The real threat to humanity is not terrorism or weapons of mass destruction but Satan the devil and the seducing doctrines of demons that manipulate the passions, desires, and fears of humanity to accomplish their goal in the world: steal, kill, and destroy. George Harkness

---

13. Lindsey, *Satan Is Alive and Well on Planet Earth*, 227–28.

explains, "The fate of [humankind] on this planet hangs in the balance between what Christ stands for and what the bomb stands for."[14] The bomb to annihilate the human race is Satan's way. Love, truth, and peace that liberate are Christ's way. The God who loves us through Christ hopes we choose the way of love because the way of Satan is to ruin the souls of people and nations. Anyone with any spiritual discernment knows that to flirt with the devil is a dangerous game of Russian roulette. Eventually, the soul will be destroyed and hopes lost. Therefore, we ought to resist the devil and put our lives in the arms of the everlasting God who loves us beyond measure.

---

14. Harkness, *Understanding the Christian Faith*, 167.

FOUR

Blind and Don't Know It

"It is possible to lead astray an entire generation, to strike it blind, to drive it insane, to direct it towards a false goal. Napoleon proved this."

—Alexander Herzen

We can all agree that eyesight is a precious gift. To be able to see the clouds, the rainbows, the birds, the trees, the flowers, family and friends is one of the great joys of life. It doesn't matter what color we are, what religion we embrace, what political party we belong to, our educational level, or any other differences we find among ourselves, all of us greatly value sight. We spend millions of dollars each year on corrective or protective lenses because we know the importance of eyesight. We want to see as much as we can as long as we can. Seeing the world and all that is in it has motivated humans to extend their eyesight. The telescope was invented to bring into view what we cannot see with the natural eye; the microscope was invented so that small or obscure object can appear larger. Satellites, space shuttles, and rockets were invented to fly outside our gravitational pull to view untold galaxies. Submarines were invented to see the depths of the ocean. X-rays machines were invented to see the inward parts of our bodies. Humans have always had this desire to see more. Among other gifts of life, seeing has brought us information about ourselves, our world, and the universe. Seeing has motivated us to light the dark places of life to make it easier to accomplish our goals and travel to our destinations. Life without sight can be very difficult and frustrating. Physical blindness doesn't mean a person is hopeless; it just means that life is more challenging. Blindness is not a death sentence. It just means one has to work harder to do things that others may take for granted.

Consider the life of Helen Keller. Although she was physically blind, she accomplished more in life than many people who could see. She graduated from college with honors; she wrote a book. She was an activist and lecturer in support of the deaf, the blind, socialism, and women's rights. She founded and promoted the American Foundation for the Blind. During her lifetime, she was regarded as one of America's most inspirational figures. Her physical blindness did not prohibit her from leaving her mark in the world. There are many people who can physically see but who are unproductive. There are many people who have 20/20 vision but cannot see beyond the natural senses. There are people who have prescription glasses but do not have insight. There are people with contact lenses but cannot see the higher principles of life. There are people who have cataracts removed but they are still spiritually blind. No matter how many times you

Blind and Don't Know It

try to explain certain facts to some people, they just don't understand. They cannot see higher ethics, higher principles, higher codes, and a higher patriotism than what they see in this material world. Blindness comes in many forms. Blindness is not just physical; it is spiritual as well.

People who are physically blind are very much aware they cannot see because darkness is all they see. They cannot see the glory of God's creation. Due to their physical blindness, they reach out for assistance to help them navigate through life. Many inventions have been developed to help improve the quality of life for the physical blind. However, spiritual blindness is different because people often are not aware of their blindness; therefore they don't think they need assistance. They see physical things clearly but cannot see spiritual things; they cannot see God's truth and revelations. Physical cataracts can be removed from the eyes to improve sight. But, James P. Gills says,

> Spiritual cataracts, however, are not so easily removed as physical cataracts. They blind us to God's purpose, making the present dim and the future unclear. The Creator of all is the only Physician who can heal this obstruction to our spiritual sight. Spiritual cataracts are outgrowths of a sinful heart, reflected in our selfishness and self-destructiveness. They are symptoms of sin and divergence from God's will and plan for us.[1]

Unless people are willing to allow God to open up their spiritually blinded eyes, they will continue to work at cross purposes with the will and purpose of God. Spiritually blinded people cannot conceive of the things of the Spirit of God. The natural man and woman do

1. Gills, *Overcoming Spiritual Blindness*, 89.

not "Receive the things of the Spirit of God, for they are foolishness to [them] nor can [they] know them, because they are spiritually discerned" (1 Cor 2:14). Therefore, it doesn't matter how educated people may be in natural knowledge and the sciences, spiritual things are foolishness to them. This is the reason the gospel of Jesus Christ was "to the Jews a stumbling block and to the Greeks foolishness" (1 Cor 1:23). The Jews and the Greeks could not understand spiritual things because they did not fall within their intellectual and philosophical system of rationalization. Their openness to the Spirit was blocked because of their distorted speculations, and human explanations that prevented their transformation. When people do not want to acknowledge God or give God glory, they become narcissists and their hearts are darkened by sin. They live and do things from a dark consciousness, which means they have become spiritually blind.

When we consciously leave God out of our thought processes and our sexuality, we work at cross purposes with the will of God. This explains how the rich can crush the poor with no remorse. This explains how the strong can destroy the weak with no conscience. This explains how sexual perversion can be displayed in the open with no shame. When we leave God out of our lives, sin takes over our thoughts, passions, and actions and we lose the capacity to discern what is right and what is wrong. As one author explains, "As long as [people see] in our present society only a few inevitable abuses and recognizes no sin and evil deep seated in the very constitution of the present order, [they are] still in a state of moral blindness and without conviction of sin."[2] Hear the apostle Paul:

2. Rauschenbusch, *Christianity and the Social Crisis*, 349.

"The natural man does not receive the things of the Spirit of God, for they are foolishness to him; nor can he know them because they are spiritually discerned" (1 Cor 2:14).

Spiritual blindness is pervasive in our nation, in the government, and in the institutions of our society. We may be instructed by what God did to the Roman Empire:

> For this reason God gave them up to vile passions. For even their women exchanged the natural use for what is against nature. Likewise also the men, leaving the natural use of the woman, burned in their lust for one another, men with men committing what is shameful, and receiving in themselves the penalty of their error which was due. And even as they did not like to retain God in their knowledge, God gave them over to a debased mind, to do those things which are not fitting; being filled with all unrighteousness, sexual immorality, wickedness, covetousness, maliciousness; full of envy, murder, strife, deceit, evil-mindedness; they are whispers, backbiters, haters of God, violent, proud, boasters, inventors of evil things, disobedient to parents, undiscerning, untrustworthy, unloving, unforgiving, unmerciful; who, knowing the righteous judgment of God, that those who practice such things are deserving of death, not only do the same but also approve of those who practice them. (Rom 1:26–31)

When God no longer exists in our hearts and minds, we are spiritually blind. Spiritual blindness causes people to deny spiritual truths or classify spiritual truths as foolishness not worthy of consideration. Therefore, people establish their own righteousness and do not "submit to the righteousness of God" (Rom 10:3). The spiritually blind cannot see that "There is a way that seems right . . . but its end is the way of death" (Prov 16:25).

Therefore, those who are spiritually blind automatically work at cross purposes with the will of God. They stifle the growth and progress of a godly society. They cause confusion and strife and plant discord among people to conserve and preserve the traditions of men and the power of the plutocrats. They join the church to promote themselves and not Jesus Christ. Moreover, spiritually blind people are dangerous. Jesus said, "They will put you out of the synagogue; yes the time is coming that whoever kills you will think that he offers God service" (John 16:2). Literally, spiritually blind people can become violent and kill, all the while thinking they are doing God service. For example, there are people in America who kill people with whom they differ philosophically, theologically, and politically; they think they are serving some good purpose. Some people think killing doctors who perform abortions serves God. We may fundamentally disagree with doctors who perform such an immoral act, but our disagreement does not give us the right to kill. Instead, we must work to change the law of the land. Too often we hear of religious extremists in foreign countries who strap bombs to their bodies and detonate them. They kill innocent people but think they have served God; as a reward for this courageous act they believe God has received them in paradise. Suicide bombings and mass killing are the results of spiritual blindness. Many people around the world are guilty of evil deeds. Ethnic cleansing and man's inhumanity to man will continue until the veil of spiritual blindness is lifted.

Blind and Don't Know It

One would think that religious people are the most spiritually insightful of all. One would think that people who attend church regularly would be the wisest and the most spiritually open-minded. To the contrary, some religious people and many who attend church are often the most spiritually blind. In Jesus day, the Pharisees were the most spiritually blind because they allowed sin to obstruct their vision of God's truth. Their envy of Jesus blinded them to the point that they called Jesus the prince of devils when they witnessed how Jesus had cast out devils (Matt. 9:34). The Pharisees hardened their hearts against Jesus and therefore remained spiritually blind. Although the Pharisees were some of the most respected religious men in Jerusalem, they loved darkness more than light. They loved power more than principle; they loved popularity more than prophetic witness; and they loved status more than the Savior. Due to their spiritual blindness these religious men formed an unholy alliance against Jesus and had him arrested and put to death. As it was done to Jesus so will it be done to all who follow him:

> Those who are in spiritual darkness are motivated primarily by anger, resentment, guilt and despair. In that state, [people] are bound toward self-destruction and defilement of [themselves] and others. [They] may become filled with a bitter, unforgiving spirit of revenge, with attempts to control and dominate others, with jealousy and lust—all obstructions to [their] vision of [God].[3]

The point here is not to argue against religion; it is an attempt to point out that if we are not careful, religion

3. Gills, *Overcoming Spiritual Blindness*, 81.

can take on a profound demonic character. People can practice religion like the Pharisees and still be spiritually blind. When religion is practiced apart from God, it can be very intolerant. For example, it is possible to practice religion that is ethnocentric which people think unless others believe and do things their way they are wrong. The Pharisees were ethnocentric in their practice of religion and because Jesus did not comply with their practice of religion, the Pharisees set out to destroy him. When the practice of religion becomes ethnocentric it leads to social, economic, and political conflict. History points out those religions have often been connected to imperialism, domination, and despotism. It has been used to enslave, oppress, exploit, and kill people. Mark O. Hatfield cautions us about the practice of a religion apart from a relationship with God:

> Let us beware of the real danger of misplaced allegiance, if not outright idolatry, to the extent that we fail to distinguish between the god of an American civil religion and the God who reveals himself in the holy Scriptures and in Jesus Christ. If we . . . appeal to the god of civil religion, our faith is in a small and exclusive deity, a loyal spiritual adviser to power and prestige, a defender of only the American nation, the object of a national folk religion devoid of moral content.[4]

Throughout history religion has been used to settle disputes and conflicts among people and nations. Unfortunately, in its efforts to settle disputes, it has not often promoted peace but war and bloodshed. Many

---

4. Hatfield, "The Sin that Scarred Our National Soul," 221.

Blind and Don't Know It

inhumane deeds have been committed in the name of religion, as Reinhold Niebuhr reminds us,

> Religion has been, in fact, so perennially involved in, and has served to accentuate, such disputes that a secular age thought it possible to eliminate the disputes by destroying religion. It failed to realize that all wars are religious wars, whether fought in the name of historic creeds or not. Men do not fight for causes until they are "religiously" devoted to them; which means not until the cause seems to them the center of their universe of meaning. This is just as true in a supposedly secular age as in an avowedly religious one.[5]

In short, the practice of religion without a relationship with God is destructive. Spiritual blindness is its by-product.

For example, look at the life of Saul who became Paul. Saul was a strict religionist who was spiritually blind. Due to his spiritual blindness, Saul persecuted the early Christians who had embraced the gospel of Jesus Christ. Christians feared Saul because he was dangerous and had a reputation of persecuting anyone who opposed the rules and regulations of Judaism: "He made havoc of the church, entering every house, and dragging off men and women, committing them to prison" (Acts 8:3). His spiritual blindness made him violent and unmerciful. He sincerely thought what he was doing was morally right. Saul continued his attacks against the church until he came in contact with Jesus Christ on the road to Damascus. When Jesus Christ introduced himself to

---

5. Niebuhr, *An Interpretation of Christian Ethics*, 210.

Saul, Saul's life changed entirely. For a while Saul lost his physical sight, and when Ananias laid his hands on Saul, "Immediately there fell from his eyes something like scales, and he received his sight at once, and he arose and was baptized" (Acts 9:18). Saul not only received his physical sight but he also gained spiritual sight. He became the greatest apostle of them all. By the grace of God, Saul's spiritual eyes were opened and he wrote most of the New Testament writings. Until people and nations receive spiritual sight, they will oppose the kingdom of God.

John Newton is another example of a man who was spiritually blind. He participated in the slave trade. He did not see that slavery was morally wrong. Spiritual blindness often eclipses our moral vision and scars our souls to the point that we do not recognize sin. When we don't recognize sin as sin, our thinking, ethics, and our practices grow corrupt. Sin not only blinds us spiritually but it also separates us from God and one another. Newton's vision was blurred because of sin. One day a violent storm arose and Newton tried to steer his ship through the storm. He thought he was going to perish. He prayed to God to have mercy upon him. Miraculously, Newton was saved, and he had an epiphany that what he was doing was wrong. He speaks about his spiritual blindness and the grace that was extended to him in one of the most loved hymns in modern times:

> Amazing Grace! How Sweet the sound
> That saved a wretch like me!
> I once was lost but now I'm found
> Was blind but now I see.

Blind and Don't Know It

Until the eyes of people come open spiritually, they will stay on the path that leads to death. Unless the veil of spiritual blindness is lifted from nations and civilizations, they will perish.

As much as we proclaim America to be a great nation, unless Americans turn to God through Jesus Christ and practices the principles Christ taught us to guide our policies and form our laws, our nation will topple and fall. Many people in America know about Jesus; many in the government and in the church say that Jesus is Lord of their lives. But as Jesus said, "Why do you call Me 'Lord, Lord,' and not do the things which I say"(Luke 6:46)? How is it that we allow money to shape our laws and pollute our land and call Christ *Lord*? How is it that politicians sell their votes to the highest bidder and call Christ *Lord*? How is it that the church, which ought to be the light of the world, allows itself to be the tail light instead of the headlight and calls Christ *Lord*? How is it that ministers of the gospel support homosexuality and same-sex marriage and call Christ *Lord*? We can love the sinner and condemn the sin; but we cannot love the sinner and affirm the sin and call Christ *Lord*. How is it that we call ourselves a Christian nation and fund an organization called Planned Parenthood where hundreds of thousands of unborn babies are aborted and call Christ *Lord*? How is it that this rich nation of ours has malnourished children and people sleeping in cars, under bridges, and on the streets when we have so many vacant buildings that could be used to assist these people and we call Christ *Lord*? When poverty and the poor are not seriously considered in our national debate, yet we call Christ *Lord*?

There is no way we can disobey the word of God and then call Christ *Lord*. There are people in the government and in the church who are so spiritually blind that they cannot see the error of their ways. If we believe and call Christ our Lord, then we must obey his word! We need to move from being *fans* of Christ to being *followers* of Christ. A *fan* of Christ is one who cheers when things are going well, when the sun is shining, and when there is a lot of excitement about the good that is taking place. But, when times become hard, and the rain of criticism begins to fall, and the excitement has been replaced with persecution, a *fan* will abandon. A follower is different. A follower is one who has made the supreme commitment to follow Christ no matter what comes. Despite adversity, confusion, setbacks, losses, and misunderstanding, a follower continues on because the follower believes that Jesus is the Way, the truth, and the life. The church as a whole must set a better example as followers of Christ; and the government must set a better example of democracy. If we claim we are a Christian nation, then our citizens are "called to an uncompromising integrity; to be true to [themselves], to truth and reality, and to Christ, no matter what other people may think or what society may want him to do."[6]

We are spiritually blind if we do not believe it is our responsibility as Christians to shape society and influence it in the right direction. Hinchliff reminds us, "A degree of political seriousness, a concern for what is happening to society, an involvement with the way it develops, is the very least we can give. Niebuhr was plainly right. A

6. Hinchliff, *Holiness and Politics*, 50.

Blind and Don't Know It

Christian who does not care about what actually happens in the political sphere, who does not lift a finger to do anything practical about it, is not really a Christian at all."[7]

Many people have argued that government cannot legislate morality, that politics and religion don't mix. Unless there is justice and righteousness in our laws and policies, God will bring judgment on our great republic. America cannot continue traveling on this course of spiritual blindness and not suffer the consequences. Corrupt politics and laws carry the seed of our own destruction. How is it that we can say on the one hand "God Bless America" and on the other hand push God out of our national life? If America has become insensitive to the immorality in the land, then the nation is doomed. It is God's people who are keeping the wrath of God from coming on America. All of our citizens ought to appreciate the Christians who are working and praying on behalf of this country. True Christians are often misunderstood, falsely labeled, and thought to be out of touch with the time and culture. Thank God there are Christians out of touch with the time and culture because if they were in touch with it, the land would perish.

Thank God we had prophets out of touch with the time and culture. Thank God we had people such as Shadrach, Meshach, and Abednego out of touch with their time and culture. Thank God we had Christians such as Peter, Paul, and the early Christians out of touch with their time and culture. Thank God we had people such as William Wilberforce, Abraham Lincoln, Sojourner Truth, Frederick Douglass, Mahatma Gandhi,

7. Ibid., 182.

and Martin Luther King, Jr. and others out of touch with their time and culture. Had these people not been "out of touch," the present might look very different. Those who truly follow Christ will always be out of touch with the time and culture to point us to a more excellent way and more loving path. God was willing to save Sodom and Gomorrah because ten righteous people could not be found in these cities. They were all spiritually blind and therefore they perished. Thank God we have more than ten righteous people in America. Let us not take for granted those people who are marching to the beat of a different drummer and traveling a different path that takes them out of the mainstream culture. The blind cannot lead the blind. Somebody has to see so we won't fall in the ditch. When we ignore and persecute those who are trying to guide us back to God and our moral foundation, we do so at our peril. Can we see that this is spiritual blindness at its worse? Can we see that divine influence is necessary for our nation's salvation? Our previous leaders believed it. George Washington did not believe that religion and politics don't mix. He said, "It is impossible to rightly govern . . . without God and the Bible. Do not ever let anyone claim to be a true American patriot if they ever attempt to separate religion from politics."[8] Washington knew the importance of God in our body politic.

Thomas Jefferson is another good example. Jefferson, although not a perfect man, understood that justice and righteousness ought to be reflected in the laws that govern us, and the thought of God's judgment made him tremble. Jefferson said, "God who gave us life gave us lib-

8. Halley, *Halley's Bible Handbook*, 18.

erty. Can the liberties of a nation be secure when we have removed a conviction that these liberties are the gift of God? Indeed I tremble for my country when I reflect that God is just, that his justice cannot sleep forever."[9] Jefferson had enough spiritual insight to know that when America becomes arrogant and removes the national conviction that God is the source of its life, liberty, and blessings, God's judgment will surely come to America. This ought to make us all tremble and repent. This ought to cause a national urgency to get the American house in order before the God of the universe thunders his displeasure upon the nation.

Although America has come a long ways and is now a multicultural, pluralistic society, it is still largely a spiritually blind nation. To our credit, Americans have created all types of advancements in science, medicine, and technology. Despite the amazing achievements in these areas, Americans still suffer from spiritual blindness. Hear the words of Martin Luther King Jr.:

> In this day of [America's] highest technical achievement, in this day of dazzling discovery, of novel opportunities, loftier dignities and fuller freedom for all, there is no excuse for the kind of blind craving for power and resources that provoked the wars of previous generations. There is no need to fight for food and land. Science has provided us with adequate means of survival and transportation, which make it possible to enjoy the fullness of this great earth. The question now is, do we have the morality and courage required to live together . . . and not be afraid?[10]

9. Notes on the State of Virginia, Query 18.
10. King Jr., "Where Do We Go from Here?" 626.

From Wall Street to Main Street

Americans ought to be outraged. Look at the present state of our nation. Look how divided our national and local governments are. Political parties cannot get anything done because they refuse to work to find common ground. They cannot put the affairs of the nation above their partisan bickering. As Thomas Paine reminds us, "Every government that does not act on the principle of a Republic, or in other words, that does not make the *res-republica* its whole and sole object, is not a good government."[11] It is a shame before God and the civilized world that many politicians would allow the nation to topple and fall instead of uniting in a spirit of cooperation to save the nation from damnation. One cannot help but agree with Sissela Bok, who stated more than thirty years ago, "Voters and candidates alike are the losers when a political system has reached such a low level of trust. Once elected, officials find that their warnings and their calls to common sacrifice meet with disbelief and apathy, even when co-operation is most urgently needed."[12]

Our government is in a spiritual crisis; our social order, too, is crumbling. One need only consider the fracture of the American family through single-parenthood and divorce. One need only look at the pervasiveness of sexual immorality in society. We have become a people without shame; indeed, the more outrageously perverse we behave, the more attention (and fame and money) we gain. We ought also to be ashamed of our skyrocketing prison population; the struggles of our schools; our crumbling highways, subways, and bridges. Any time we

---

11. Paine, *Common Sense and Other Writing*, 201.
12. Bok, *Lying: Moral Choice in Public and Private Life*, 175.

Blind and Don't Know It

value profit over human life, comfort over caring for others, greed over generosity, sales over sensitivity, famous life above family life, political party over principles, self-centeredness over other-centeredness, and materialism over spirituality, the soul of America is on the verge of being lost. Jesus said, "What profit is it to a man [a woman, and a nation] to gain the whole world and then lose [one's] soul" (Matt 16:26)?

Americans' spiritual blindness is so pervasive that very few people heed our spiritual crisis. America is in serious moral and economic trouble. Cornel West describes America's crisis this way:

> America is a first-class military power becoming a second-class economic power and in a stage of cultural decay and decline. Think about that—tremendous military power, but losing more and more economically to the Japanese and West Germans and others, and culturally you can't walk the streets at night. That's decay. It's decline. It's deterioration. It's a high level of criminality and so forth and so on.[13]

How can Americans really enjoy our lives and freedoms when our communities are held captive by criminality? How can we teach children sexual responsibility when sexual immorality is omnipresent in the media and on our handheld devices? Satan fills our air with anything that opposes God. The American culture is becoming so anti-God, anti-morality, anti-traditional-family those who live according to God's word and the spiritual principles are sometimes vilified and ostracized. John Hagee

---

13. West, *Beyond Eurocentrism and Multiculturalism*, 205.

brings into focus what is happening in our nation. He made this very cogent observation:

> When our government condones what God condemns, those who have trusted in Him are labeled dangerous, "intolerant," and enemies of the state.... Christian bashing is already an art in the popular media. Christians are the only group in America that it is politically correct to hate, discriminate against, and lampoon. We are attacked through the law, through the media, through Hollywood, and through educational institutions that belittle the Word of God and traditional family values.... Today in most American public schools you can distribute condoms, teach lifeboat ethics, and affirm that it's normal for Heather to have "two [lesbian] mommies," but you can't read the Bible.... The Supreme Court has ruled that it is unconstitutional for the Ten Commandments to be posted on a classroom wall. Why? Because students might read them and the words might affect their moral character. Heaven help us, for in a generation marked by drive-by shootings, murder, rape, teenage suicide, drug abuse, homosexuality, pornography, and Satanism, we certainly wouldn't want to affect moral character development! "Political correctness" is the new commandment foisted on all children.[14]

The spiritual blindness of America is its greatest threat. Turning our backs on the Creator is the worst sin a nation can commit, and no political party, economy, or military might is sufficient to provide security for us in the future. Until Americans understand that "Righteousness exalts a nation but sin is a reproach to any people" (Prov

14. Hagee, *Beginning of the End*, 123–24, 126–27.

14:34), there is no future of life, liberty, and the pursuit of happiness for future generations. The spiritually blind do not see and understand that "We shall reap what we sow."

There is nothing that prevents us from doing what is right and just for this nation. We don't do what is right because we don't have the will, which is a feature of spiritual blindness. Out of all the blindness we find in our world, spiritual blindness is the worst. As James Gills explains, "Our greatest sin before God may be our refusal to acknowledge the Lord's hand in our existence, to be grateful for it, and the One responsible for our existence, everything else in life is shrouded in darkness and ignorance–then we are blind."[15] When a nation shuts its eyes to God's will and way, what hope is there for the future? Gills continues, "Until we have abandoned our egos, independence, and self-serving inclinations at His feet, we have nothing and we remain blind."[16]

---

15. Gills, *Overcoming Spiritual Blindness*, xvi.
16. Ibid., 249.

FIVE

The Toll of Gun Violence

"America is a workshop of death." —Walter Rauschenbusch

We hear about gun violence daily in America. Killings occur every day in communities across the nation, especially in urban areas where gangs and guns are a way of life. We hear about gun violence in schools and now in churches. We have become a nation at war with itself. There is no question that if Americans don't get a handle on the crisis of gun violence, we will destroy ourselves. How many more breaking news stories from places like Columbine High School, Virginia Tech, Colorado, and Newtown will it take before Americans demand stronger and more effective gun control laws? According to the Brady Center to Prevent Gun Violence, "Our nation suffers from an epidemic of gun violence. Guns take the lives of 105 Americans every day—15 of them are children and teenagers.... Sensible national gun control laws are urgently needed to stem this violence."[1]

1. Haerens, *Gun Violence*, 131.

The Toll of Gun Violence

Too many people, especially our youth, are losing their lives because Americans have not made this epidemic a top priority. Are we truly indifferent to the 30,000 thousand deaths that occur every year due to gun violence?

America is the most armed nation in the civilized world. It is estimated that 3,000 guns are manufactured per day in the Unites States. Per one hundred citizens in America, 89 own guns, which gives America the highest gun ownership in the world. It is sad that more isn't being done on the federal level to stem the epidemic of gun violence on our streets, workplaces, schools, and homes. Some argue that we have enough gun regulation, but laws are no stronger than their enforcers. What is the use of having laws we do not enforce? Guns that were made for soldiers in combat should not be for sale in the general population. It doesn't make sense for AK-47 assault rifles to end up in the hands of criminals and gangs. If the government doesn't aggressively enforce gun regulations, our national security is at risk, and more innocent victims will fall prey to this deadly epidemic.

There is no question that Americans have the right to bear arms; it is our Second Amendment right to do so. The question is not "Do we have the right to bear arms?" The question is "Do we have the right to kill to settle our differences and satisfy our pathology with guns?" It is the responsibility of the government to enforce gun regulation and create stricter laws if necessary to preserve American life. If terrorists killed Americans at the same rate that Americans kill one another, our government would be highly motivated to deal with those terrorists. What is our responsibility to the families of the 30,000 thousand Americans lost each year to gun violence? Should we continue to argue about the rights to bear arms, or is it our moral obligation and responsibility to do something about the proliferation of guns and gun violence? What is it going to take for us to put public safety before politics and responsibility before profit?

National leaders of both political parties have failed to work for consensus concerning gun control to make our communities safer. When a problem is consistently neglected, or we refuse to face it, we must pay the price. We have untold losses in the untapped potential of men, women, and children who have been lost to gun violence. What else might people such as Abraham Lincoln, John F. Kennedy, Robert Kennedy, Martin Luther King Jr., and John Lennon contributed to our national culture had they lived? We can only speculate about the potential lost in Newtown, Connecticut, where an entire class of children was lost. What would have been the contributions of those future leaders, scientists, teachers, doctors, ministers, mothers, fathers who were lost that day? We will never know.

According to the Brady Center to Prevent Gun Violence "Over a million people have been killed with guns in the Unites States since 1968, when Dr. Martin Luther King, Jr. and Robert F. Kennedy were assassinated."[2] What kind of nation would America be today had these people lived? Think of the people you know who were killed by gun violence and the contributions they could have made to the world had they lived. The more we refuse to confront this problem, the more

2. Kevin Ahern, "Confronting Our Culture of Violence," July 20, 2012.

The Toll of Gun Violence

we diminish the greatness of our nation and put public safety at risk.

Gun violence is taking away the greatest asset a nation can have: children. If for no other reason, we ought to create a society that protects children and youth from gun violence. We ought to build the kind of nation we all want our children and grandchildren to live in. Young people cannot aspire to their highest potential in school and in the community when the noise of gun shots fills the air. When people are afraid to come out of their homes because of gun violence, their quality of life is reduced significantly. When children are afraid to play outside, they miss opportunities to forge bonds in and with their communities. We cannot build a strong nation when community life is stunted by the fear of violence.

Not only does gun violence stifle the quality of life in our nation, it is also driving up health care costs. The number of victims who come into the emergency care units across the nation is staggering. Who pays for emergency health care for gunshot victims? We all do in one way or another. We have failed to teach our children conflict resolution; without peaceful means to resolve our differences, we will never have a more perfect union. Conflict resolution will help create public safety and make our nation a moral example of people who can disagree without becoming violently disagreeable. Unless we learn how to settle our differences without aggression, we will plunge our nation and the world into yet more darkness. If Americans want to lead in democracy, we must show the world how to settle differences through nonviolent means at home. Martin Luther King Jr. warned us that

"We must learn to live together as brothers and sisters or together we will be forced to perish as fools."[3]

If we can come together and put a man on the moon, send rockets into space, swim the depths of the oceans with sophisticated submarines, and put a rolling computer on Mars, why can't we unite to find a solution for gun violence? If protecting the sacredness of life is not our top priority, what are we looking for in space? Our problem is here on earth. Our job is to do the will of God on earth as it is in heaven. And, it is the will of God that the sacredness of life is protected. It is the will of God that we create the kind of society where children can live and grow and contribute to the life of the nation that would glorify God. To create this kind of society, we must listen and heed what Jesus told his disciples: "Blessed are the peacemakers for they shall be called the children of God" (Matt 5:9). We must work for peace for the public good. The flame of hostility can be extinguished by peacefully working for peace. We can preserve our nation and give succeeding generations the opportunity to live in a country where gun violence is a thing of the past, but we must commit ourselves to peace. This means we must do more than discuss gun control in the wake of senseless gun violence and then go back to business as usual when the story is no longer front-page news. We must make a daily commitment to work for peace in our everyday dealings with each other. Jesus said to his disciples, "Put your sword in its place, for all who take the sword will perish by the sword" (Matt 26:52). Notice here that Jesus said "Put your sword in its place." Jesus understood that the

3. King Jr., *Where Do We Go From Here: Chaos or Community?*, 171.

The Toll of Gun Violence

sword has its place only to be used when peaceful means have been vigorously pursued and exhausted. Jesus understood that there are other ways to resolve conflict; we ought to seek those alternative ways.

There is no reason we cannot do better in this area in America. We can create a society that employs conflict resolution before we take up the gun on each other. There is no reason we cannot protect the sacredness of life in the nation we love. What use are the words of life, liberty, and the pursuit of happiness in the great Constitution of our nation if we refuse to enforce commonsense legislation to safeguard life, liberty, and the pursuit of happiness. We are not true patriots of America when we participate in the destruction of life that we claim to protect. When gun assess is easy and laws are not as tight and enforced as they could be, we are not honoring the spirit of the Constitution. Consider the words of Eric W. Alexy: "The problem with guns seems to be the same as tobacco, booze and any other killer of thousands that makes billions: If it makes money, the likelihood of common sense taking precedence over dollar signs is close to nil, thus negating any chance of a nationwide ban on firearms ever happening."[4]

If making money is our idol above everything else in life, then it just may be that this idol will destroy America. Arnold Toynbee stated, "An instrument that has once been used to destroy life cannot then be used to preserve life at the user's convenience. The function of weapons is to kill. . . . The man of violence cannot both genuinely repent of his violence and permanently profit

4. Haerens, *Gun Violence*, 105.

by it."[5] Americans must repent! Gun violence is a malignant cancer on America. To ignore it is our peril. Like ignoring cancer in the body that can eventually destroy the body, ignoring gun violence on the city streets of our nation will destroy our great republic—socially, morally, and economically.

The goal is not to demonize the Second Amendment. The goal for us is to consider the senseless proliferation of guns; how they are being used on American citizens; and how we can stop guns from getting into the hands of people who should not have them. Guns such as assault weapons are made for the military and should not be allowed in our communities. When we allow guns of this magnitude on our streets, they often get in the hands of people who should not have them. We jeopardize the safety of the public and the police officers whose duty it is to protect us. Collectively, we have to put pressure on our legislatures and demand that they do a better job protecting the American public from the proliferation of guns and assault weapons. In an editorial James Atwood stated that we must struggle against gun violence with a holy rage:

> One of the most loving things one can do to prevent violence, or honor those who have needlessly suffered and died, is to welcome a holy rage. When violence is destroying human beings, those who love are enraged. When injustice reigns, rage is often the first step of love. Jesus was angry when worshipers were exploited in the temple. In an act of love he turned over tables and threw out the moneychangers.

5. Douglass, "The Nonviolent Cross," 217.

The Toll of Gun Violence

> William Wilberforce, member of the English Parliament, was enraged by the cruelty of the slave trade. With love in his heart he went public in his denunciation and became a major figure in the abolitionist movement. Sojourner Truth was so angry over the indignities of slavery that with insightful love she walked thousands of miles to help slaves "follow the drinking gourd" to freedom. When Dutch Christians witnessed Nazi atrocities against Jews, they were outraged and started smuggling Jews to safety. Freedom riders were incensed "the colored" could not eat at lunch counters in five-and-ten cents stores, sit in the front of the bus, or use toilets in gas stations. Out of love for their brothers and sisters, they boarded buses and helped break the chains of segregation. People who love do not sit back and watch when terrible things are happening to neighbors or friends. Those who love welcome within a holy rage.[6]

Ultimately, we must ask ourselves, *What kind of nation do we desire?*

Some argue that it is *people* who kill—not guns. Dorothy Anne Seese a freelance political writer for Patch Work and columnist for Ether Zone said,

> Guns are instruments, neutral, they do not go on shooting rampages. People do. They use the guns for wrong purposes. The same is true of irresponsible drivers, corrupt officials, and drug dealers. Drugs don't wander around looking for someone to sniff them or smoke them or inject them. People sell drugs to people willing to do these things. The blame is always, always, always

6. Atwood, "Bringing Down Violence with Holy Rage."

> and forever on the people, not the objects they use.[7]

Although we can see some validity in this argument, the fact remains that guns are the instruments of choice, and they cause more deaths than any other instrument of choice. The United Methodist Church agrees that "While guns are not the sole cause of violence, their ready availability for purchase, easy accessibility to children, and convenient access to those contemplating criminal activity or suicide make gun violence a monumental social problem."[8] Stopping the proliferation of guns, taking out of circulation assault weapons, and making it harder for people to obtain guns can help people to resolve conflict another way. Unless we act to prevent gun violence, the social fabric of our nation will continue to be torn apart. Our nation doesn't have to be seized by violence and trepidation that leave children dead on the streets and families paralyzed by fear in their homes. As one Christian organization recommended,

> We can turn away from violence; we can build communities of greater peace. It begins with a clear conviction: respect for life. Respect for life is not just a slogan or a program; it is a fundamental moral principle flowing from our teaching on the dignity of the human person. It is an approach to life that values people over things. Respect for life must guide the choices we make as individuals and as a society: what we do and won't do, what we value and consume, whom we admire and whose example we follow, what we support and what we oppose. Respect for hu-

---

7. Haerens, *Gun Violence*, 142.
8. "Gun Violence in the U.S.," 537.

The Toll of Gun Violence

man life is the starting point for confronting a culture of violence.[9]

There is no question what gun violence is doing to our nation. However, there are some things we can do to reduce gun violence in America. It is going to take each and every one of us to play our part for greater public safety and the common good. Here are some fundamental things we can do:

- Vote for politicians who favor stricter gun laws;
- Challenge our national leaders to enforce gun control laws and create greater consequences for violating these laws;
- Encourage parents to teach nonviolent conflict resolution in the home by modeling civil and respectful conversations;
- Support regulations that require that guns have safety locks and are kept from the reach of children;
- Require conflict resolution education in schools;
- Refuse to support through ticket sales or media purchases the studios who glorify violence in their productions;
- Encourage pastors and other religious leaders to discuss gun violence more often from their pulpits and other venues to show how peace is the path God wants us to travel;
- Work with community organizations to combat social and economic injustice that creates conditions

[9]. Unites States Conference of Catholic Bishops, "Confronting a Culture of Violence."

of poverty and powerlessness where gun violence grows;

- Encourage the media to cover positive news stories where people are making a difference in creating a less violent society. The more we see and hear of the good work others are doing across the nation, the more people are willing to get involve to make our nation safer.

We will not be able to eradicate all violence, but we must never give up the struggle to create a more peaceful world. James Atwood puts America on notice:

> The Gun Empire carries within the seeds of its own destruction, particularly in its classic overreach and promotion of violence. As it seeks more power through devious means and grasps for more exclusive privileges, it sets in motion undeniable and unconquerable spiritual forces that will inevitably lead to its own defeat. Its outrageous methods will eventually bring about its own demise. It will die as all Empires die, by claiming way too much."[10]

America must find a way to end its national love affair with violence. The more war and violence we create, the more hunger and disease we cause. In the words of Dwight D. Eisenhower, "Every gun that is made, every warship launched, every rocket fired, signifies in a final sense a theft from those who hunger and are not fed—those who are cold and not clothed."[11]

---

10. Atwood, *America and Its Guns*, 204.
11. Loeb, *Soul of a Citizen*, 289.

The Toll of Gun Violence

Violence may occupy a place on the throne for a while but it must give way to peace because Jesus Christ is the Prince of Peace. Peace will eventually rise out of the blood of the slaughtered because the Lord has spoken it. The Lord has said through the prophets Isaiah and Micah, "They shall beat their swords into plowshares, and their spears into pruning hooks; nation shall not lift up sword against nation, neither shall they learn war anymore" (Isa 2:4; Mic 4:3). One day peace will prevail. Peace should be our goal, the commitment of all of our aspirations.

SIX

When a Nation Forgets God

"When you have eaten and are full, then you shall bless the Lord your God for the good land which He has given you. Beware that you do not forget the Lord your God by not keeping His commandments, His judgments, and His statutes which I command you today, lest when you have eaten and are full, and have built beautiful houses and dwell in them; and when your herds and your flocks multiply, and your silver and gold are multiplied, and all that you have is multiplied; when your heart is lifted up, and you forget the Lord your God ... and follow other gods ... you shall surely perish" (Deut 8:10–14, 19, NKJV).

There is an old saying, "Those who forget the lessons of history are doomed to repeat them." We should have learned from history that it is suicidal to leave God out of the scheme of things. Jim Wallis makes a cogent point about history in relation to America. He said,

> History teaches us that when the gap grows between the rich and the poor, when the middle gets increasingly squeezed, and those at the bottom are almost forgotten, a crash is about

When a Nation Forgets God

> to come.... Our religious traditions do indeed point the way: in times of relatively shared prosperity, there are no biblical prophets, because they are not needed. But when inequality is on the rise, the prophets rise up to thunder the judgment and justice of God. The God of the Bible seems not to mind prosperity—if it is shared. But, when it is not, God gets angry. And when wealth becomes more and more concentrated, bad things begin to happen to us: social bonds begin to unravel, societal morale erodes, and resentment sets in when we perceive great unfairness.[1]

When God is left out of our national life, selfishness, greed, and pride set in. We forget "the earth is the Lord's and they that dwell therein" (Ps 24:1). When a nation's citizens forget God, the poor are crushed and the needy are neglected and forgotten.

America is increasing becoming a secular society. It has become a strange land where people and values have drastically changed. Years ago there were some things we thought would not happen in America, but this is no longer the case. Fifty years ago who would have thought that 9/11 would happen in America? Who would have thought that the younger generation would be dying sooner than the older generation? Who would have thought that there would be more men in prison than in colleges and universities? Who would have thought that single-parent homes would out number two-parent homes? Who would have thought that America would have the highest divorce rate in the world? Who would have thought that the cost of living would be what it is

1. Wallis, *Rediscovering Values*, 82.

today? Who would have thought that gas prices would this high today? Who would have thought that the federal government would endorse same-sex marriages? Who would have thought that people today would not be ashamed of their abominations?

Erwin W. Lutzer stated, "Back in the 1970s Francis Schaeffer told us that one day we would wake up and discover that the America we once knew was gone. One does not have to be a prophet to see that dark days are coming to the United States."[2] Judgment is coming because we are busy escorting God out of our national life. We are substituting godless ingenuity for divine guidance. We have removed the Ten Commandments from government buildings and courthouses; we have banned Bible reading and prayer from public schools. We have given approval for same-sex marriage, which is clearly contrary to the will of God. We have killed millions of children by abortion; we reward the rich and punish the poor and needy. In the name of freedom we have endorsed indecency, abomination, and wantonness in our children. We have thrown out spiritual values. Americans have forsaken their sacred heritage and wonder why our nation is in the mess it is in.

Massey Mott Heltzel, one of President Eisenhower's favorite preachers, made a very convincing observation about what we should remember about Germany's downfall:

> We do well to remember what happened in Germany. . . . Germany's sense of right and wrong, its ideals of justice and truth, were not

2. Lutzer, *When a Nation Forgets God*, 12.

When a Nation Forgets God

the first to go; rather, the foundation facts, the belief in the saving deeds of God, were the first loss. Not long after the rise of Hitler, an American minister was talking with Dr. Emil Brunner, one of the foremost theologians on the continent of Europe. The American said: "It seems almost unbelievable that Germany, with its long Christian tradition, a nation that has given the world many of its greatest spiritual leaders, should so soon have turned from the faith of the fathers and become pagan." Dr. Brunner answered: "Ah, that is where you make your mistake. The paganism of Germany was no sudden thing. For over half a century God and religion have been disappearing from the schools of Germany. Education has become secular. A generation has arisen which acknowledges no God and no longer regards those basic moral sanctions which are the foundation of national and international harmony and decency." First, there was no acknowledgment of God, and then the disregard of moral sanctions! Religion went first, and ethics were sure to follow! When people lose sight of what God has done, they soon lose sight of what they ought to do. When man's relationship to God is wrong, his relationship to man can never be right—well, for a while, perhaps, but not for long.[3]

Are not we seeing the same trend in America? What happened to Germany will also happen in America if our citizens refuse to repent. There are forces at work trying to completely wipe God out of the nation. The more we wipe God out, the more we wipe out morality and righteous values that are necessary for the survival of a nation. The

3. Heltzel, *Best Sermons*, 101.

more we remove God from public places, the more God is forgotten and no longer part of our consciousness. The greatest danger is moving God out of our hearts. When God no longer occupies a place in our hearts, we are like coldblooded creatures that devour one another. Pay close attention to what God told Ezekiel concerning Israel: "Because you have forgotten Me and cast Me behind your back, therefore you shall bear the penalty of your lewdness and your harlotry" (Ezek 23:35). This can be applied to America. Our nation has cast God behind its back and will reap some painful consequences. Could it be that all of the natural disasters, the economic downturn in our economy, the national debt, etc., are signs that God is rescinding his protection from America? Once God removes his covering of protection, devastation, sorrow, and distress are the consequences. All of our riches cannot save a nation under God's judgment. All of the policies both domestic and foreign, cannot save a nation that has forgotten God. It may well be that God's judgment is upon America. If God punished ancient Israel for its sin and evil, beware! God is no silent onlooker; do not be complacent that God won't do the same to this nation.

Like America, the nation of Israel was blessed beyond measure. They were blessed because God was their leader; God was their provider; God was their protector; God was their deliverer and their salvation. The people of Israel were blessed because they had the God of the universe on her side. We cannot get better protection, better provision, better deliverance, better salvation, and better blessings than what the Lord provides. When we have the Lord we have all that we need to be a successful and prosperous nation. The children of Israel were a blessed

When a Nation Forgets God

nation of people. All they had to do was to bless the Lord and obey his commandments. He brought them from slavery to royalty, from oppression to liberation, from obscurity to visibility. Doing their forty years in the wilderness they never went hungry; they never went thirsty; they never were attacked by enemies; they never were bitten by scorpions, and their clothes and shoes never wore out. God was good and faithful to Israel. All God asked of them was to remember that it was the Lord who had given them all these blessings.

God gives us memory for a purpose. When we remember, we stay humble. Kenneth Waters reminds us of the importance of memory: "When we remember, we stay rooted. When we remember, we stay grounded. When we remember, we stay strong. When we remember, we stay connected. When we remember, we stay balanced. When we remember, we stay whole."[4] There are continued blessings toward us when we remember it is the Lord who has provided. We know who we are and whose we are when we remember. When we forget, as Israel did and as America is doing, the consequences can be catastrophic. Martin Luther King, Jr. stated,

> Without dependence on God our efforts turn to ashes and our sunrises into darkest night. Unless [God's] spirit pervades our lives, we find only what G. K. Chesterton called 'cures that don't cure, blessings that don't bless, and solutions that don't solve.' . . . like many [people] of the twentieth century became so involved in big affairs and small trivialities that [they] forgot God."[5]

4. Waters, Sr., *Afrocentric Sermons*, 72.
5. King Jr., *Strength to Love*, 73.

God saw the danger of prosperity and cautioned the children of Israel:

> Beware that you do not forget the Lord your God by not keeping His commandments, His judgments, and His statutes which I command you today, lest—when you have eaten and are full, and have built beautiful houses and dwell in them, and when your herds and your flocks multiply, and your silver and your gold are multiplied, all that you have is multiplied; when your heart is lifted up, and you forget the Lord your God who brought you out of the land of Egypt, from the house of bondage. (Deut 8:11–14)

In other words, God was saying to the children of Israel, "Don't allow your prosperity to cause you to forget the Lord who delivered you, who blessed you, who protected you, who fed you, who watched over you. Don't allow your prosperity to become a curse for you because as sure as you forget the Lord, you will surly perish." Unfortunately, the children of Israel forgot the Lord. They allowed their prosperity to become their distraction and curse, and they bowed to gods of pleasure and materialism. They paid a heavy price. God warned the nation of Israel not to walk contrary to his way and commandments:

> Then, if you walk contrary to Me, and are not willing to obey Me, I will bring on you seven times more plagues, according to your sins. I will also send wild beasts among you, which shall rob you of your children, destroy your livestock, and make you few in number; and your highways shall be desolate. And if by these things you are not reformed by Me, but walk

> contrary to Me, then I also will walk contrary to you, and will punish you yet seven times for your sins. And I will bring a sword against you that will execute the vengeance of the covenant; when you are gathered together within your cities I will send pestilence among you; and you shall be delivered into the hand of the enemy. ... And after all this, if you do not obey me, but walk contrary to Me, then I also will walk contrary to you in fury; and I, even I, will chastise you seven times for your sins. (Lev 26:21–28)

It is dangerous and deadly to walk contrary to God. Like ancient Israel, America has forgotten the Lord and is walking contrary to the will of God. We have replaced moral value for market value. We have substituted the common good with greed. We have forgotten that our country's founders, although imperfect, established a Christian nation who included God in its government. Alternative marriage is now socially acceptable, along with sexual immorality in all forms of media. The Christian values and standards we once embraced are now being mocked as being out of step with the times. Money, sex, pleasure, and power have become our idols. Jim Wallis writes that,

> Our society has promoted the cultural sin of covetousness, which offers either enormous opulence or the experience of vicarious wealth through watching the opulent on television. We have created an industry of voyeurism, with reality TV shows holding up the wrong kind of heroes and teaching us to strive to be just like them.[6]

---

6. Wallis, *Rediscovering Values*, 44.

Instead of being each other's keeper, we have adopted the Darwinian concept of the survival of the fittest in which the strong survive and the weak perish. The Judeo-Christian values we once made a part of our national and social life have been thrown out by the new market values of greed, selfishness, and pride. We no longer concern ourselves with the plight of our neighbors.

Due to political correctness our government no longer seeks divine guidance. Erwin W. Lutzer writes,

> When God is ousted from government, transcendent values are replaced by the raw use of power, eroticism, arbitrary judicial rulings, and the morality of personal pragmatism. Without overarching absolutes, the unity of society is threatened in the face of fragmentation and the request for personal "rights." Civility, long a characteristic of American life, has degenerated into name-calling and a desire to destroy the opposition. As Dostoevsky has famously said, "When God does not exist, anything is possible." Political correctness has now affected the general culture and created an aura of censorship and a climate of fear.[7]

Because of our pride and arrogance, instead of saying, "Our Father which art in heaven hallowed be thy name thou Kingdom come, thou will be done on earth as it is in heaven," we are saying, "Our brethren which art upon the earth, hallowed be our name. Our kingdom come. Our will be done on earth, for there is no heaven."[8] America has forgotten the God of our weary years and the God of our silent tears.

---

7. Lutzer, *When a Nation Forgets God*, 27.
8. King Jr., *Strength to Love*, 72.

When a Nation Forgets God

We want God to bless America all while we have escorted God out of public places; thrown out God's precepts and commandments, and made a mockery of justice. Rev. Joe Wright made a profound observation. He said,

> We have ridiculed the absolute truth of [God's] Word and called it pluralism. We have worshipped other gods and called it multiculturalism. We have endorsed perversion and called it alternative lifestyle. We have exploited the poor and call it the lottery. We have rewarded laziness and called it Welfare. We have killed our unborn and called it choice. We have shot abortionists and called it justifiable. We have neglected to discipline our children and called it self-esteem. We have abused power and called it politics. We have coveted our neighbor's possessions and called it ambition. We have polluted the air with profanity and pornography and called it freedom of expression. We have ridiculed the time-honored values of our forefathers and called it enlightenment.[9]

Of course this kind of public truth is labeled "politically incorrect" to hide or be in denial about how far we have moved away from God.

There is no doubt about it our land is spiritually and morally sick. Many of our leaders are corrupt, our public schools are corridors of shame, our prisons are bursting at the seams, churches are quiet and complacent, and our families are dysfunctional. We do not live in a post racial society because racism has raised its ugly head in

---

9. Wright, Prayer in Kansas House of Representatives, http://www.eaec.org/desk/joe_wright_prayer.htm.

the highest form of government. It is a sad commentary in the life of this nation that we can come together to fight in foreign lands and cannot come together to solve problems in our own land. Until we put our lives, our families, schools, churches, and social institutions back into spiritual perspective, America's fate will be no different from the decline and fall of the Rome Empire. When we forget the Lord, we automatically enter into a time of decay and destruction. We enter into a time of trouble and uncertainty. The greatest problem in America is not Washington, DC; it is not the economy; it is not racism, sexism and terrorism; it is not the liberal left versus the religious right. These are problems, but they are not the greatest problem. Our greatest problem as a nation is spiritual anemia. We have forgotten the Almighty God. God has faded out of memory for many of the American people.

Unless Americans return to God, tragedy and failure could befall us at any time. We are not insulated as we thought we once were. We have a choice today. Come back to God or see the painful death of our great republic. Read the relevant words of Martin Luther King, Jr. to America:

> America, I wonder whether your moral and spiritual progress has been commensurate with your scientific progress. It appears to me that your moral progress lags behind your scientific progress, your mentality outdistances your morality, and your civilization outshines your culture. How much of your modern life can be summarized in the words of your poet Thoreau: "Improved means to an unimproved end." Through your scientific genius you have made of

When a Nation Forgets God

> the world a neighborhood, but you have failed to employ your moral and spiritual genius to make of it a brotherhood. So, America, the atomic bomb you have to fear today is not merely that deadly weapon which can be dropped from an airplane on the heads of millions of people, but that atomic bomb which lies in the heart of [people], capable of exploding into the most staggering hate and the most devastating selfishness. Therefore I urge you to keep your moral advances abreast of your scientific advances.
>
> I find it necessary to remind you of the responsibility laid upon you to represent the ethical principles of Christianity amid a time that popularly disregards them.... Your highest loyalty is to God. ... If any earthly institution or custom conflicts with God's will, it is your Christian duty to oppose it. You must never allow the transitory, evanescent demands of man-made institutions to take precedence over the eternal demands of the Almighty God.[10]

King, along with others with spiritual discernment, knew that America was drifting toward paganism, and there would be a price to pay for it. Just because God's judgment hasn't totally come to America doesn't mean it won't. God's delay is not God's denial. God is giving America a chance to return to Him to do His will on earth as it is in heaven.

Regardless of how ugly things are in America, our nation can once again become America the beautiful if we turn our hearts back to God and one another. We cannot snatch our nation back from the brink of destruction without God in our hearts and without the cooperation

---

10. King Jr., *Strength to Love*, 139–40.

of one another. We need each other to save our nation. Reaching out to one another and across racial, political, economic, and denominational lines is necessary to put our nation back in line with the will of the God. Our differences ought to be our strength. Erwin W. Lutzer stated,

> Today in America we need an army of ordinary heroes to stand against the gathering darkness in our land. We need people who will stand for truth courageously, consistently, and with humility and grace. We need millions of believers who will represent Christ in the various vocations of America. We need to enlist people who know what they believe, why they believe it, and how to live out their convictions in diverse situations. We need those who are willing to pay the price of discipleship and obedience and do so with joy. A tall order, but possible.[11]

To help our nation chart the course back to God, we must start in our homes. We must teach our children to fear God and to keep his commandments. Our children need to know that God is the core of all life and knowledge. All that is begins with God. If we cannot put God back into education, America is doomed for sure. We would do well to heed the words of Carolyn Caines on the definition of true education:

> If I can learn my ABCs, can read 600 words per minute, and can write with perfect penmanship, but have not been shown how to communicate with the Designer of all language,
>
> I have not been educated.

---

11. Lutzer, *When a Nation Forgets God*, 118.

When a Nation Forgets God

If I can deliver an eloquent speech and persuade you with my stunning logic, but have not been instructed in God's wisdom,

I have not been educated.

If I have read Shakespeare and John Locke and can discuss their writings with keen insight, but have not read the greatest of all books—the Bible—and have no knowledge of its personal importance,

I have not been educated.

If I have memorized addition facts, multiplication tables, and chemical formulas, but have never been disciplined to hide God's Word in my heart,

I have not been educated.

If I can explain the law of gravity and Einstein's theory of relativity, but have never been instructed in the unchangeable laws of the One Who orders our universe,

I have not been educated.

If I can classify animals by their family, genus, and species and can write a lengthy scientific paper that wins an award, but have not been introduced to the Maker's purpose for all creation,

I have not been educated.

If I can recite the Gettysburg Address and the Preamble to the Constitution, but have not been informed of the hand of God in the history of our country,

I have not been educated.

From Wall Street to Main Street

> If I can play the piano, the violin, six other instruments and can write music that moves men to tears, but have not been taught to listen to the Director of the universe and worship Him,
>
> I have not been educated.
>
> If I can run cross-country races, star in basketball, and do 100 push-ups without stopping, but have never been shown how to bend my spirit to do God's will,
>
> I have not been educated.
>
> If I can identify a Picasso, describe the style of da Vinci, and even paint a portrait that earns an A+, but have not learned that all harmony and beauty comes from a relationship with God,
>
> I have not been educated.
>
> If I graduate from high school with a perfect 4.0 and am accepted at the best university with a full scholarship, but have not been guided into a career of God's choosing for me,
>
> I have not been educated.
>
> If I become a good citizen, voting at each election and fighting for what is moral and right, but have not been told of the sinfulness of man and his hopelessness without Christ,
>
> I have not been educated.
>
> However, if one day I see the world as God sees it and come to know Him, Whom to know is life eternal, and glorify God by fulfilling His purpose for me,
>
> then I have been educated.[12]

12. Carolyn Caines, "To Be Educated" Reprinted with permission from BJU Press.

When a Nation Forgets God

As Israel could not function without God, neither can America. We need to believe and sing again in our hearts the old hymn that is so true: "Without Him I can do nothing, without him I would fail; Without Him my life would be rugged. Like a ship without a sail.[13] When a nation forgets God it can do nothing but fail and great shall be the fall of it.

If America decides not to include God in its national life, like the nursery rhyme "Humpty Dumpty," it will have a great fall, and no one will be able to put America back together. We are on the verge of falling. When we neglect the poor and turn a deaf ear to the needy, we are on the verge of falling. The nation's wealth is in the hands of two percent of the people. Ninety-eight percent of the people are suffering from a lack of jobs and opportunity, but this economic injustice cannot last forever. When Americans ignore the voices of the prophets of old who thundered against greed, injustice, oppression, and the neglect of the "least of these" great shall be the fall of America. When God breaks the backbone of a nation who under heaven can put that nation back together? Americans must turn from pride and arrogance, greed and oppression. Like the prophet Daniel said to the King of Babylon, "We have been weighed in the balances, and found wanting" (Dan 5:27). The nation's downfall is at hand. Abraham Lincoln said it best:

> We have been the recipients of the choicest bounties of heaven. We have been preserved, these many years, in peace and prosperity. We have grown in numbers, wealth and power, as

13. Mylon R. LeFevre, African American Heritage Hymnal 2001, 515.

no other nation has ever grown. But we have forgotten God. We have forgotten the gracious hand which preserved us in peace and multiplied and enriched and strengthened us; and we have vainly imagined, in the deceitfulness of our hearts that all these blessings were produced by some superior wisdom and virtue of our own. Intoxicated with unbroken success, we have become too self-sufficient to feel the necessity of redeeming and preserving grace, too proud to pray to God that made us! It behooves us, then to humble ourselves before the offended Power, to confess our national sins, and to pray for clemency and forgiveness.[14]

---

14. Lincoln, "Proclamation for a National Day of Fasting, Humiliation and Prayer," Proclamation 97.

SEVEN

Lost Values

"Your beliefs become your thoughts; your thoughts become your words; your words become your actions; your actions become your habits; your habits become your values; your values become your destiny."

—MAHATMA GANDHI

In these capitalistic, materialistic, and hedonistic times in which we live, our nation has lost many of its very important core values that once kept America morally strong. The new normal values are replacing traditional core values. The new values of greed, individualism, and out of control spending that is creating a mountain of debt are not bringing us together but tearing us apart. Jim Wallis stated,

> The new maxims, "Greed is good," "It's all about me," and "I want it now" have replaced old virtues. Being number one is now more important than anything or anyone else and has become even more important than the One who will ultimately hold us all accountable. A market

> based on greed and fear has tugged on some of the worst things in us, and we are now paying the consequences.[1]

Casting aside many of our traditional core values has stifled our national progress and arrested our greatness. The core values that used to bind us together as a nation have unraveled, and we find ourselves at war with each other. Marriages and families are breaking up like never before. We have lost our sense of community; we have lost respect for one another; we have lost our ability to agree to disagree. We label one another; we live outside our means; and we treat one another as enemies rather than neighbors. Republicans and Democrats view cooperation as weakness. As a nation we have already gone off the cliff; we have gone off the cliff of immorality; the cliff of corruption; the cliff of ungodliness; the cliff of arrogance; the cliff of being outright rebellious against God, justice, and righteousness.

We need to reestablish those core values that made America the greatest nation in the world. This is not to suggest that America was ever perfect. We have our share of flaws. Our core values provided at least the framework for us becoming a "more perfect union." Our national ideal of being "One nation, under God, indivisible, with liberty and justice for all" was grounded in our core values. Once upon a time, we took ownership of our freedom, worked hard, played by the rules, and continued the struggle of believing in America the beautiful.

Once upon a time, nations of the world looked to America as a model of freedom and opportunity. What

1. Wallis, *Rediscovering Values*, 43.

Lost Values

was it about America that people around the world saw us as a land of opportunity? What was it that made us proud to be Americans? What was it that brought out the better angels of our nature? These are the questions we need to ask ourselves to discover where we went wrong. Jim Wallis continues,

> We need to find where we made our wrong turns and how we got off track; then we need to face the truth. Our country has had times of great prosperity when the rich, the poor, and everyone in between enjoyed the fruits of their labor. Not all our old habits, behavior, and institutions are bad, just as not all new ones are good. We need to uncover some forgotten lessons that have served us well in the past and make sure the baby of our choices doesn't get thrown out with the bathwater of our mistakes.[2]

When we stopped practicing our core values, or worse, replaced them with new normal values of greed, individualism, and out of control spending, we faced a decline and lost respect in the eyes of the world. We need to rediscover our lost values.

One lost value we need to rediscover is the importance of family. The breakdown of the family is contributing to our national moral decay. There was a time when families worked together, struggled together, dined together, worshipped and prayed together. Parents parented their children and set the code of conduct for them to follow. Parents were the thermostats of their homes and community. Unfortunately, today this has changed. Too many parents have become thermometers allowing

2. Ibid., 6–7.

themselves and their children to register the behavior and culture around them. Instead of leading their children, they are befriending their children. Children need parents who will guide them and set expectations—and hold them accountable when the expectations are violated.

A generation ago this is what most parents did. They held children accountable for their character and behavior. They believed in the biblical teaching that parents ought to "Train up a child in the way he should go, and when he is old he will not depart from it" (Prov 22:6). In the family we learned how to deal with others in society; we learned values such as respect, discipline, responsibility, unity, hard work, honesty, sharing, conflict resolution, and living within our means. Schools and churches reinforced these Judeo-Christian values. The family, the church, and the schools were three institutions that collaborated and supported one another; this collaboration made us a better community and therefore a better nation. There were rarely high school dropouts, youth going to prison, gun violence, youth funerals, drug use, and teen pregnancies. Education was understood as a way to better oneself. It was not uncommon to hear "Yes, sir," "No, sir" "Yes, ma'am," and "No, ma'am." These were respectable forms of address to parents and elders.

Moreover, irresponsible behavior was not rewarded in the family, school, or the church. Corrective steps were taken to help children learn from mistakes. Through discipline and other restricting measures, children learned what was expected and how to make wiser decisions. When families had a strict standard, most children lived up to them. But, as time moved on there was a dramatic turn in the way children were raised. Parents allowed

Lost Values

secular views to creep into their way of raising children. As Stephen L. Carter explains,

> Sadly, many children grow up in an atmosphere in which the character building institutions are quarreling instead of cooperating. Many families no longer have time for teaching the young how to behave. . . . As to the place of worship, fewer and fewer children attend one with any regularity. . . . When children do go to church, some traditions seem to have abandoned interest in suggesting that God may actually have given us rules by which we are to live.[3]

Today, too many parents say, "We don't want to raise children like we were raised." But, if we adhered to the values our parents raised us with and we turned out fine, why do we think children today won't do likewise? Children need guidance and structure today just as they did a generation ago—perhaps more. Yes, parents were tough on us; yes, parents made sure we understood the expectations, and yes, parents did not spare the rod. Children were disciplined at home and at school. Without these lessons, we may understand why many youth are self-destructive; why many are disrespectful; why many are having children out of wedlock; why many are dropping out of school; why many are learning to depend on public assistance; and why many are dying far too young. They have not learned to respect themselves or those in authority over them. As their parents expected less of them, they learned to expect less of themselves. Perhaps this explains the behavior of Wall Street and Main Street. Whenever we decide to abandon core values, the nation

---

3. Carter, "Civil Reactions," 53.

suffers. Whatever seeds we allow to be sown, we shall reap them. We are helping to put a financial strain on society. Children born out of wedlock require more public funding than children from two-parent homes. Children who get into trouble and end up in prison require more public funding. One way or another, we are all paying for the our collective failure to instill moral values in children to teach them to contribute to society. As a result, they are draining society of its resources. Ben Carson makes a profound observation

> I believe one of the reasons our nation prospered was a strong emphasis on traditional family values that included instruction on a difference between right and wrong, teaching that began in the home and continued at school. And one of the central sources for defining values was the Bible, which back then was found in all public schools. Basic religious principles were taught in public schools in such a way as to have the broadest possible application without favoring any particular denomination. Children were taught that there was a Creator to whom they were responsible and that there was a moral code given to us by the Creator to whom we would all have to answer in the afterlife. . . . When I was a child, it was generally considered shameful to have a child out wedlock, whereas today, in many segments of our society, having a child out of wedlock is the norm, not in any way assigned social stigma. Many people feel this indicates that we are progressing to a more enlightened stage and that we are less judgmental and more accepting of everyone. Although being open-minded and accepting is a good

Lost Values

thing, we should examine the effects this change in attitude has on society as a whole.[4]

Parents are not making demands on children like they once did and irresponsible behavior is rewarded more than not. Whenever we reward irresponsible behavior, the burden of doing so gets heavier and heavier on society. We understand that people make mistakes, but to keep on making the same mistakes over and over again cannot be good for a democracy. The nation can be no greater than the families who live in it. Many of our great leaders, such as President Harry Thurman, Martin Luther King Jr., etc., made reference to what they learned within family that provided the ethical framework and guidance that helped them to lead and succeed. Family is the backbone of the nation, and when the family is in a crisis, the nation is in a crisis. Rediscovering the importance of family and the biblical principles that provide guidance can help heal and turn the nation around.

Another value we must rediscover is a sense of community. We must realize we need each other. To make honey takes more than one bee; to gather enough food for winter takes more than one ant; to wipe out a crop takes more than one grasshopper; to build a bridge takes more than one man; to make an automobile takes more than one employee; to win a war takes one than one soldier; to transform a nation takes more than one citizen; to advance the kingdom of God takes one than one Christian. We need each other. God designed community to let us know that we were not made to travel life alone; we were not made to walk life alone, work alone, watch alone, wait

4. Carson, *America the Beautiful*, 105.

alone, weep alone, and witness alone. John Donne wrote, "No man is an island entire of itself. Every [person] is piece of the continent; a part of the Maine."[5] Life is not designed for us to shoulder the problems of the community by ourselves. When we understand our need for one another, we can make America a better nation.

The Apostle Paul describes the need for community by comparing it to the human body. Paul says,

> If the whole body were an eye, where would be the hearing? If the whole body were hearing, where would be the smelling? But, now God has set the members, each one of them, in the body just as he pleased. And if they were all one member, were would the body be? But now indeed there are many members, yet one body. And the eye cannot say to the hand, I have no need of you, or again the head to the feet; I have no need of you. (1 Cor 12:14–27)

We need each other in the community whether we realize this or not. Only if we can understand our need for one another, can we make the world community a better place. Martin Luther King Jr. said,

> We do not finish breakfast without being dependent on more than half the world. When we arise in the morning, we go into the bathroom where we reach for a sponge which is provided for us by a Pacific Islander. We reach for soap that is created for us by a Frenchman. The towel is provided by a Turk. Then at the table we drink coffee which is provided for us by a South American, or tea by a Chinese, or cocoa

---

5. Donne, *Devotions upon Emergent Occasions*, Mediation 17.

Lost Values

by a West African. Before we leave [our homes] we are beholden to more than half the world.[6]

Another value we must recapture is good stewardship. America is living far outside of its means. Consumerism is causing more people to be buried in debt. America's debt is out of control and if we don't get a handle on our national debt, generations to come will not enjoy the quality of life that we have enjoyed. We must get our financial house in order. There should be fair taxation to run the country, fund schools and social programs, and eliminate government waste. People who handle and mismanage public and private funds should be held accountable because mismanagement affects us all. Spending and looking for someone else to pay the bill is not only morally wrong but the height of selfishness. The American people—and politicians in particular—need to read again the wisdom of Jesus who said, "For which of you, intending to build a tower, does not sit down first and count the cost, whether he has enough to finish it" (Luke 14:28). Before we spend, we ought to sit down and count the cost. America has moved away from counting the cost. We are putting the burden on the next generation, which is not only unfair but undemocratic. How can we leave our children and grandchildren an inheritance when we are deeply buried in debt? It is irresponsible to burden the next generation that did not create the problem.

Another value we need to rediscover is the spirit of civility in our society. Our democracy cannot last long when we treat each other the way we do. Our national

6. King, Jr., *Strength to Love*, 70.

leaders have lost the spirit of civility and hold the nation captive because they refuse to put the welfare of the nation above their personal feelings. When we lose civility, we lose the capacity to work together. Our leaders and society have become so disconnected that caring about people seems to be abnormal. The conditions of poverty and hopelessness don't move us with a sense of urgency. If the debt crisis and the welfare of this nation were really a top priority for our leaders, they would cooperate to bring America out of the crisis. The fracture between the people and its government is causing suffering; people are feeling left out, neglected, and forgotten. Sociologists tell us that when people feel they have no stake in society, when they feel hopeless, they are more likely to become anti-social and destructive. We must make a conscious choice to become more civil in all of our interactions with one another; this is the only way to rediscover our caring society.

We must work for social change and set goals with a clear vision. Our goals must be formed with the good of the whole country in mind. The first question then is what should be the goal of society? Henry Hughes, a nineteenth-century sociologist stated that society has two ultimate ends: "The first end of society is the existence of all." Everybody in society ought to be able to live life. The second goal of society "is the progress of all." Everybody ought to be able to progress in society and be given equal access to capital, education, health care. Hughes goes on to say that a "Society is an organization. . . . A society organization is therefore a union of seven organs for seven ends. These are the economic system, whose organic end is the subsistence of all." He continues,

Lost Values

> The political system, whose organic end is the security of all.
>
> The hygienic system, whose organic end is the health of all.
>
> The philosophic system, whose organic end is the education of all.
>
> The esthetic system, whose organic end is the enjoyment of all.
>
> The ethical system, whose organic end is the morality of all.
>
> The religious system, whose organic end is the religion of all.[7]

We cannot reach the goals that Henry Hughes described without God and the core values that made us a strong nation. Because we have abandoned God and most of our values, media outlets carry news on a daily basis about our increasingly decadent society. The hearts of people have become cold; they don't care if their actions or inaction affect others. They don't care what they do to cause suffering. Predatory lenders don't care if people lose their houses or if there is turmoil in the housing industry. Some CEOs don't care if their mismanagement will cause the loss of thousands of jobs. Drug dealers don't care about taking the lives of others. Our society is moving from one level of cold bloodedness to another. Unless we go back and include the Almighty God in our national life and practice the core values that made us strong, America will never rise up and live out the true meaning of its creed.

---

7. Hughes, *Treatise on Sociology Theoretical and Practical*, 47–49.

From Wall Street to Main Street

As Gandhi said, "Your values become your destiny." If we have the wrong values, our destiny will be destructive. If we discover the values that work well for us, then our destiny will be good and prosperous. It is up to us which destiny we desire. "If our goal is to go back to business as usual, we will soon be right back to what got us here in the first place. To go back to business as usual would be to miss the opportunity this crisis provides to change our ways and return to some of our oldest and best values."[8]

Martin Luther king, Jr. said it best, "I am convinced . . . we as a nation must undergo a radical revolution of values. We must rapidly begin the shift from a "thing-oriented" society to a "person-oriented" society. When machines and computers, profit motives and property rights are considered more important than people, the giant triplets of racism, materialism, and militarism are incapable of being conquered. A true revolution of values will soon cause us to question the fairness and justice of many of our past and present policies. . . . an edifice which produces beggars needs restructuring."[9] The hour is late and it is time for America to make a paradigm shift in its values. Our democracy depends on it. We have a choice today to reclaim the values that made us strong, responsible, and humane, or embrace new values of greed, callousness, and apathy that will ultimately destroy us. It is my hope that America chooses the former rather than the latter.

---

8. Wallis, *Rediscovering Values*, 5.

9. Martin Luther King, Jr., "A Time To Break Silence," in *A Testament of Hope*, Ed. James Melvin, 240–41.

Conclusion

There Is Hope for America

"Learn from yesterday, live for today, hope for tomorrow."
—Albert Einstein

Wisdom of the past has taught us that "Only when it gets dark enough can we see the stars," and "If mountains were smooth we could not climb them." This is to say regardless of how dark our times are and severe our crisis may look, there is still hope for America. Our nation can make a great turn around. Although America has gotten off the moral and spiritual track, it can get back on track. Morality and democracy can still be the stock and trade of our nation. It is going to take the will of "We the People" to get America back on track heading toward God's forgiveness and restoration. Americans need to repent before God and acknowledge the error of their ways. Acknowledgement of error is good, but it must be followed by corrective action. It is not enough to arouse the conscience of the nation; efforts must be taken to transform the conscience of the nation. America needs spiritual transformation. Our fundamental problem is not social, political, or economical but spiritual. Until we first fix our spiritual problems, we will never be able to solve our national problems. Americans have become so distracted by the cares of this world that they have lost touch with the spiritual. They have become indifferent toward God and spiritual matters. In order to have renewal in America, we must reconnect with our best, spiritual selves. Without a lifeline to God, American democracy cannot survive. Democracy needs a taproot grounded in the soil of spirituality to keep it from dying when it is seriously challenged. Jesus told us centuries ago, "I am the vine, you are the branches. He who abides in Me, and I in him, bears much fruit; for without Me you can do nothing" (John 15:5, NKJV). Therefore, "Spirituality is first. Without it, education will turn into a striving after the wind, culture into lasciviousness, social transformation into social unrest, philanthropy into sprinkling of rosewater over the carcass."[10]

Our spiritual condition in America is an indicator of why our social and economic life is in jeopardy. If there is no striving toward God, there will be a downward spiral of morality. When there is a downward spiral of morality, the national situation degenerates into corruption. The nation drifts further and further to greater depths of vice and ruin threatening the future stability of the nation. America is spiritually feeble, and until America is healed spiritually the media will continue to carry news of tragedy after tragedy. Dread and despair will continue to flood the streets of America until we can take no more;

10. Rauschenbusch, *Selected Writings*, 70.

then "We the People" will reach out to God for social and cultural change. There will be such an outcry for change, a great spiritual revival for the transformation of society will be sparked. This spark will grow to ignite a desire to regain those noble principals that made the nation great and prosperous. The answer is in the moral and spiritual struggle. Until Americans are willing to reestablish the values that made the nation great, anti-God and anti-democratic forces will continue working against us.

There have been forces at work to destroy what good people have built up in America. Despite the legacy of slavery, racism, injustice, and corruption that kept the nation from becoming a more perfect union, there have been good people who have worked to make our nation better and more humane. These people have come in all shapes, sizes, and colors. They worked hard for the social regeneration of the nation. They did not agree all the time, but they knew that the common good of the nation was at stake. They were spiritually grounded enough to cooperate without compromising their moral and spiritual convictions. Whenever the nation faced a crisis, they knew that silence and inaction were not options. They pressured our leaders to act, and by acting they made America a better nation for all people.

We need to regain the spirit of cooperation to save America. The moral, spiritual, social, and economic crisis we are in demand our cooperation. The future of the nation is at stake. The crisis in America is so severe that it touches all of us in one way or another. How does it touch us all? When a window of a house is broken, the house is not condemned. The window can be repaired. When the roof of a house is damaged, the house is not condemned.

From Wall Street to Main Street

The roof can be repaired. When the pipes of a house burst, the house is not condemned. The pipes can be repaired. But, when the foundation of the house is cracked and crumbling, the house is condemned. It is useless to repair a house when the foundation is crumbling. This is to say that the foundation of America is under attack, and unless ordinary Americans come together and save the foundation of this great republic, the foundation of morality, the foundation of democracy, the foundation of family, the foundation of justice, the foundation of decency, and the foundation of the education and protection of our greatest asset our children, the foundation on which America rests is condemned. It is going to take all of us who truly love this nation and what it offers to come together across racial, economic, and religious lines to save America. We come together in times of war to save and protect our American interests; what greater interest can there be than to save and protect the foundation of the nation? The saving of our nation cannot be deferred. We must act now because there may not be an opportunity later. We may not get to the Promised Land in our generation, but we must make steps to come out of the Egypt of our present situation.

We need leaders who are not thermometers that register the temperature of society, who just go along to get along. We have far too many leaders of this type. The time for thermometer leaders is over. We need *thermostat* leaders who are not afraid to set the temperature of society. We need leaders who have moral convictions and who are not afraid to bring these convictions to bear on the economic, social, and political life of the nation. We need leaders to give encouragement and strength to the

There Is Hope for America

spiritual life of the nation and inspire us to have faith in our efforts to help the nation chart another course. From the local, state, and national level, we need leaders who understand that "Righteousness exalts a nation"—not the government, not military power, not a strong economy, not technological advancements, but righteousness. When leaders and the people understand that they must do what is right and just toward God and one another then there is hope for America.

If "We the People" can work to save the sacred heritage of our nation, we can repair the windows of opportunity, the roof of justice and equality, fix the economy, ensure the pipeline of fairness to all people, and deliver to the next generation a much more morally, socially, and economically sound nation. But, this change must come from the people, from the bottom up. Woodrow Wilson made a very cogent observation. He said,

> Everything I know about history, every bit of experience and observation that has contributed to my thought, has confirmed me to the conviction that the real wisdom of human life is compounded out of the experiences of ordinary [people]. The utility, the vitality, the fruitage of life does not come from the top to the bottom; it comes, like the natural growth of a great tree, from the soil, up through the truck into the branches to the foliage and the fruit.. A nation is as great, and only as great, as her rank and file. It behooves the nation to remember that a people shall be saved by the power that sleeps in its own deep bosom, or by none; shall be renewed in hope, in conscience, in strength, by waters welling up from its own sweet, perennial springs. Not from above; not by patronage of its

> aristocrats. The flower does not bear the root, but the root the flower. Everything that blooms in beauty in the air of heaven draws its fairness, its vigor, from its roots. Nothing living can blossom into fruitage unless through nourishing stalks deep-planted in the common soil."[11]

If America is to regain the beauty of its democracy, its leadership in the free world, and its respect around the globe, the common efforts of the people must move upward through the soil of their struggle to demand leadership from its leaders.

America has faced dark times before, and the nation came through it for the better because the people worked, struggled, and sacrificed to make it happen. American history is a history of struggle and sacrifice, and those who struggled knew there was a Force that aided and strengthened their efforts. This Force is still available to work in and through us to save our nation again from those who want to bury our democracy and sacred heritage in the same hopeless grave. This Force is God. God through Christ is our light: "Because this light is always and everywhere immanent, ready to reveal itself, our religious traditions remind us that we're never completely alone and forsaken. However much human destructiveness can ravage individual lives, communities, and even ecosystems, it cannot destroy the fundamental source of life and, thus, of hope."[12]

Dwight D. Eisenhower's words are as relevant today as they were when he spoke them. Speaking to the nation he said, "We must not permit present problems to form

11. Wilson, *Light from Many Lamps*, 313–14.
12. Loeb, *Soul of a Citizen*, 336.

There Is Hope for America

a wall of bewilderment that shuts off our view of great futures. The future is the special province of the young, of you and your companions throughout the land! Schooled in the lessons of the past, [unafraid] by the present, you look ahead with confidence."[13]

So, our hope is in returning to God who blessed our nation beyond measure. Our hope is replacing idols with the true and living God. Once we replace the idols with the true and living God, we will begin to see moral and spiritual healing of the nation. We cannot do this just by praying for situations and circumstances to change. Prayer is crucial, but it cannot substitute for action. Listen to the words of Abraham Lincoln and Frederick Douglass, who helped America to chart a different course in its national history. When the nation was in a crisis and thick darkness of uncertainty hovered over our great republic, Lincoln said, "With malice toward none, with charity for all, with firmness in the right as God gives us to see the light, let us strive to finish the work we are in, to bind up the nation's wounds, to care for him who shall have borne the battle, and for his widow and his orphans, to do all which may achieve and cherish a just and lasting peace among ourselves and with all nations."[14] In an effort to help move the nation away from slavery and injustice and establish democratic principals for all people Frederick Douglass said,

> Greatness does not come on flowery beds of ease
> to any people. We must fight to win the prize.
> No people to whom liberty is given can hold it
> as firmly and wear it as grandly as those who

13. Eisenhower, *Light from Many Lamps*, 296.
14. Douglass, *Life and Times of Frederick Douglass*, 363–64.

> wrench their liberty from the iron hand of the tyrant. The hardships and dangers involved in the struggle give strength and toughness to the character, and enable it to stand firm in storm as well as in sunshine.[15]

These two giant personalities knew that inaction and indifference were not options. To save America again, justice must override profit, principals must override politics, perseverance must override fatigue, and faith must override hopelessness.

Yes, America is in deep trouble, and, yes, we are on the edge of a social and economic cliff. But, renewal and redemption are always an option for a nation at a crossroads. We just have to make sure we select the right road to travel. The road of normalcy or business as usual will certainly bring about America's demise. The road of repentance will invoke God's grace and mercy and we may be spared because of our repentance. God may still bruise America, but grace and mercy may keep the nation from being broken. One thing is for sure, America's future is determined by her citizens. And, if we sit back and allow what offends God to continue, then we cannot weep and wail when our country has fallen.

The hope that was prescribed to ancient Israel is still available to America. Our hope is in the prescription that comes from God who said, "If My people who are called by My name will humble themselves, and pray and seek My face, and turn from their wicked ways, then I will hear from heaven, and will forgive their sin and heal their land" (2 Chr 7:14). But, it demands action on our part. We as a

---

15. Ibid., 505.

There Is Hope for America

nation must do our part by repenting of our national sins and putting God back on the throne of our hearts. The healing of America, the stability of its economy, and the longevity of its future are all contingent upon the private and social morality of the nation. Out of the chaos of our dark times, God can bring order and command light to shine to guide us through the maze of our present crisis. There is hope for America! The choice is ours.

Bibliography

Ahern, Kevin. "Confronting Our Culture of Violence," July 20, 2012, http://dailytheology.org.

Armstrong, Herbert W. *The Incredible Human Potential*. Philadelphia: Church of God Punishers, 2004.

Atwood, James E. *America and its Guns: A Theological Exposé*. Eugene OR: Wipf & Stock, 2012.

———. "Bringing Down Violence with Holy Rage." July 3, 2012 Posted by Kurt Willems, http://www.patheos.com/blogs/thepangeablog.

Bedell, George C., Leo Sandon, Jr.; Charles T. Wellborn, *Religion in America*. Second Edition, New York: Macmillan 1982.

Bok, Sissela. *Lying: Moral Choice in Public and Private Life*. New York, New York, Harvester Press, 1978.

Bonhoeffer, Dietrich. *Creation and Fall*. New York: Simon & Schuster, 1997.

Buber, Martin. *Hasidism*. New York: Philosophical Library, 1948.

Caines, Carolyn. "To Be Educated" Reprinted with permission from BJU Press.

Carson, Ben. *America the Beautiful: Rediscovering What Made This Nation Great*. Grand Rapids: Zondervan, 2012.

Carter, Stephen L. "Civil Reactions." *Christianity Today* Vol 45 issue 9, July 9, 2001): 53.

Donne, John. Devotions upon Emergent Occasions, Meditation 17, 1624. The Works of John Donne. Vol III. Henry Alford, ed., London: John W. Parker, 1839. 574–75.

Douglass, Frederick. *Life and Times of Frederick Douglass*. New York: Macmillan, 1962.

Douglass, James. "The Nonviolent Cross." In *Christian Peace and Nonviolence: A Documentary History*. Edited by Michael G. Long. New York: Orbis Books, 2011.

Bibliography

Foluke, Gyasi A. *The Real Holocaust: A Wholistic Analysis of the African-American Experience, 1441–1994*. New York: Carlton Press, 1995.

Gills, James P. *Imaginations*. Lake Mary, FL: Creation House, 2004.

———. *Overcoming Spiritual Blindness*. Lake Mary, FL: Creation House, 2005.

"Gun Violence in the U.S." The Book of Resolutions of the United Methodist Church, 1996. Tennessee: United Methodist Publishing House, 1996.

Haerens, Margaret, editor. *Gun Violence: Opposing Viewpoints*. Farmington Hill, MI: Greenhaven Press, 2006.

Hagee, John. *Beginning of the End*. Nashville: Thomas Nelson, 1996.

Halley, Henry H. *Halley's Bible Handbook*. Grand Rapids: Zondervan, 1962.

Harkness, Georgia. *Understanding the Christian Faith*. Nashville: Abingdon-Cokesbury Press, 1947.

Hatfield, Mark O. "The Sin that Scarred Our National Soul." *Christian Century* 90/8 (February 1, 1973): 221.

Heltzel, Massey Mott. *Best Sermons*. Edited by G. Paul Butler. New York: McGraw-Hill, 1955.

Hinchliff, Peter. *Holiness and Politics*. Grand Rapids: Eerdmans, 1982.

Hughes, Henry. *Treatise on Sociology Theoretical and Practical*. Philadelphia: Lippincott, Grambo & Co., 1854.

Kendall, R. T. *Jealousy: The Sin No One Talks About*. Lake Mary, FL: Charisma House, 2010.

King, Martin Luther Jr. *Strength to Love*. Philadelphia: Fortress Press, 1963.

———. "Where Do We Go from Here?" In *A Testament of Hope*. Edited by James Melvin Washington. New York: Harper & Row Publishers, 1986.

Lasch, Christopher. *The Revolt of the Elites and the Betrayal of Democracy*. New York: W.W. Norton & Company, 1995.

Lincoln, Abraham. "Proclamation for a National Day of Fasting, Humiliation and Prayer," April 30, 1863, http://www.abrahamlincolnonline.org/lincoln/speeches/fast.htm.

Lindsey, Hal. *Satan Is Alive and Well on Planet Earth*. Grand Rapids: Zondervan, 1972.

Loeb, Paul Rogat. *Soul of a Citizen Living with Conviction in a Cynical Time*. New York: St. Martin's Griffin Press, 1999.

Lutzer, Erwin W. *When A Nation Forgets God*. Chicago: Moody Publishers, 2010.

Mays, Benjamin. *Quotable Quotes*. New York: Vantage Press, 1995.

Bibliography

Milton, John. *Paradise Lost*. Edited by Gordon Campbell. New York: Alfred A Knopf, Publisher, 1992.
Munroe, Myles. *The Burden of Freedom*. Lake Mary, FL: Charisma House Publishers, 2001.
Niebuhr, Reinhold. *An Interpretation of Christian Ethics*. New York: Meridian Books, 1956.
Notes on the State of Virginia, Query 18, 1781, http://www.thefederalistpapers.org.
O'Brien, John A. *Truths Men Live By*. New York: Macmillan, 1946.
Paine, Thomas. *Common Sense and Other Writings*. New York: Barnes & Noble Classics, 2005.
Phillips, J. B. *God Our Contemporary*. New York: Macmillan, 1960.
Phillips, Kevin. *American Theocracy*. New York: Penguin Group, 2006.
Rauschenbusch, Walter. *Christianity and the Social Crisis*. New York: MacMillan, 1907.
———. *Selected Writings*. Edited by Winthrop S. Hudson. New York: Paulist Press, 1984.
Smith, Huston. *World's Religions: A Guide to Our Wisdom Traditions*. New York: Harper San Francisco, 1991.
Thurman, Howard. *Jesus and the Disinherited*. Richmond, IN: Friends United Press, 1981.
Tillich, Paul. *The Religious Situation*. Translated by H. Richard Niebuhr. New York: Meridian Books, 1956.
Unites States Conference of Catholic Bishops, "Confronting a Culture of Violence: A Catholic Framework for Action," 1994, United States of Catholic Bishops, http://www.usccb.org.
Wallis, Jim. *Rediscovering Values*. New York: Howard Books, 2010.
Warren, Rick. *The Purpose Driven Life*. Grand Rapids: Zondervan, 2002.
Washington, James Melvin, editor. *A Testament of Hope The Essential Writings of Martin Luther King, Jr*. San Francisco: Harper & Row Publishers, 1986.
Waters, Kenneth L. Sr., *Afrocentric Sermons*. Valley Forge, PA: Judson Press, 1993.
Weatherhead, Leslie D. *The Will of God*. Nashville: Jove Publications for Abingdon Press, 1944.
West, Cornel. *Beyond Eurocentrism and Multiculturalism*. Volume 2. *Prophetic Reflections: Notes on Race and Power in America*. Maine: Common Courage Press, 1993.
Wieman, Henry Nelson. *Creative Freedom*. New York, New York, The Pilgrim Press, 1982.
Wilberforce, William. *Real Christianity*. Ventura, CA: Regal Books, 2006.

Bibliography

Wilson, Woodrow. *Light from Many Lamps*. Edited by Lillian Eichler Watson. New York: Simon & Schuster, 1951.

Wright, Joe. Prayer in Kansas House of Representatives, January 23, 1996, http://www.eaec.org/desk/joe_wright_prayer.htm.

www.ingramcontent.com/pod-product-compliance
Lightning Source LLC
Chambersburg PA
CBHW071438160426
43195CB00013B/1948